Black Butterfly; White Rose

Transformed

by

Cathy McDade Franklin

TDR Brands Publishing

Formatting and Editing by Rafael Allen Romasanta III

Published by TDR Brands Publishing

Formatted and edited by Rafael Allen Romasanta III

ISBN: 978-1-947574-33-5

Table of Contents

Love Letter

My Dearest Sister,

May I begin by asking you to inhale…. Exhale… Take a look at yourself in the mirror – do you see that beautiful woman looking back at you? Oh, how I can relate to the deliberate attempts made by the enemy to tear you down, cause you to "see yourself" as less than - less than others… Beloved, may I ask of you to look at your hands – clench them tightly. Inhale…. Exhale… NOW, RELEASE those closely tightened fists into the air! Today, make an intentional promise to yourself that you will no longer clench your fists – from this day forward, you will walk in freedom! You are free from anger, destructive thinking, and from any form of influence that has driven you to a negative outcome, verbal response, or action.

My sister, you are the most precious being, and God loves you. I love you, and I am grateful that you have allowed me into your personal space. It is my earnest prayer that this book will help enlighten you; as I share pieces of me with you, may it be received with a heart that knows Christ died on Calvary so that you can live an abundant life. Never allow the subtle darts of the enemy to rob you of what was given to you freely!

Are you ready for your release?

Are you really ready?

Ok, then let's agree together – Father, in the name of Jesus, I repent for owning the worry, images, and emotional torture from my past! The hound of horror in hell has been found out. Today, God, I release my faith to receive healing. I recruit the presence of the Holy Spirit, and I welcome a refresh of my anointing. God, you said in 1 Peter 5:7 that I can cast all my cares upon you, and that you care for me! Today, I receive your gift of carefree living – I will not consume the worries from my past, and I decree that I am now transformed into the woman that you called me to be. May I walk in my blessing in a way that edifies Your Kingdom and brings You Glory – from this day forward; with open arms, I embrace You in Your fullness. In the name of Jesus, Amen.

Exodus 33:14 *"And He said, 'My Presence will go with you, and I will give you rest.'"*

Preface

I begin by giving God who made the Heavens and the earth all the praise! Father, in the name of Jesus – thank You for using me as a vessel to share my life's experiences for the edification of Your Kingdom! From a teachable spirit to the

Luke 5:10

"...And Jesus said unto Simon, Fear not; from henceforth thou shalt catch men" (KJV).

Master Teacher, may You be glorified by the reader of this book, may You be seen, may Your voice be heard, and may many receive salvation as a result of what you speak to their hearts. It is through You, Father, that I have this opportunity, and I do not take my task lightly. Holy Spirit; Ministering Angels – I yield my gates of knowledge and my fingers to you; together we will complete this assignment. I invite you into the most intimate details of my life – the darkest moments; the numbing suicidal moments: the moments carved through the pain and suffering from child-abuse and neglect, childhood anger and rage, becoming a mother at fourteen, surviving a domestic violence relationship, and multiple marriages. I also invite you into my current state and I encourage you to travel with me on this journey with an open mind – reserving judgment. According to 2 Corinthians 1:3-7, the apostle Paul shares that the compassion and comfort from God given to us during our troubles should be extended to those who also suffer. I believe that my assignment isnot only to share my life with you but also to share the Good News! Thank you for allowing me into the canvas of your mind; may I ask of you to hone in on healing and begin the process of transforming as you prepare to release the toxic images of your past.

A caterpillar (who crawls around on the lowest parts of the earth) morphs into a butterfly by stuffing itself with leaves, by growing plump and long, and by shedding its skin.The caterpillar eventually stops eating, hangs upside down from a twig or a leaf and spins itself a cocoon. Within its protective casing, the transformation of its body begins with the caterpillar digesting itself, releasing enzymes to dissolve all of its tissue. Once disintegrated, a protein-rich substance is used to fuel the cell division required for the butterfly's body to develop so that it can fly freely andbeautifully, so that it can sow into the earth by pollinating plants and flowers to produce new seeds. I love this analogy of transformation because it offers a different perspective on how we transition during our times of vulnerability, and how our transformation is intentional – our transformation is intended to "produce new seeds".

Part 1:

Generational

Curses

Chapter 1:

Who Do You Say I Am?

Oreo. Zebra. White girl. Confused. Freckleface. Wild hair. Crooked teeth. Whoa – wait, I can hear you! I am a little girl… Fragile in heart... Vulnerable, and in the most influential stages of my life… Be careful, please. Take care of me. Protect me, Daddy! Nurture me, Mommy – please! I am depending on you to give me what I need to transition from your nest into this big world, so please be patient with me as I learn who you are, what family is and who I am to become as I am evolving into a woman.

I was a little girl looking for love, acceptance, and a healthy upbringing. I was looking to grow up as a normal little girl with dolls, tutu's, dresses, tea sets, play dates, and childhood friends, friends whom I would keep in touch with throughout college and into my adulthood years. We would be each other's bridesmaids, watch each other have children, raise our children together. We would watch our children go off to college, we would retire and take international vacations as couples – but there's one problem...

I don't know the person that you say I am!

From the heart of a little girl, you are molding my self-image and tainting how I view myself... You have influenced me with the wrong behaviors and you've left me in the dark to search for my true identity. Mommy! Daddy! Where are you? Make it stop! Please... The dreams, the night sweats from horror, the hand slap, make it all stop. But wait, you're no longer here... What's happening? Who am I? Am I who you say I am? NO!

Chapter 2:

Who Are You?

When I began this project, I was embarrassed about what people would think if they knew me... I mean – if they REALLY knew me! What's more interesting is that I was afraid of how I would view myself once I uncovered layers of scarred tissue; but the truth is, this is a part of my healing journey. However, my inquisitive nature couldn't resist the urge to "self-inquire," Cathy:

- Are you weak?
- Unfortunate?
- Still searching?
- What's your motive, girl...?

These are all great questions – so let's explore their answers... I've invited you into my life because I believe that you may be suffering in many of the same areas in which I have suffered, or that you know of someone who is. Let's share, shall we... Don't think of it as strange if you reply verbally while reading – let's just say you're responding to the Holy Spirit. Go on, smile – it's OK at this point. God is about to reveal something inside of you, and I yield to my assignment as the vessel used to open the door – isn't He so cool! During our time together as you read about my experiences, it is my prayer that you will close the most painful chapter in your life, and that you will rest in your cocoon as you begin to transform into who God has called you to become.

Has anyone ever told you, "Girl, you are so *dysfunctional?"* After hearing it so much, you become marked - and like a lightning bolt – you now own that image. Dysfunctional. Well, angelheart – by the aid of the Holy Spirit, let me help you - that is not your identity. According to Genesis 1:27 *"God created man in His own image; in the image of God He created Him; male and female He created them"* (NKJV).

You are strategically crafted – every detail of your being has been carefully placed to be as it should. So, clap your hands, Cover Girl, and do your happy dance… In fact, take a minute or two – check yourself out in the mirror! Those beautiful eyes are custom artwork! That nose, your lips, your ears, your hair texture, your eyebrows, your skin tone, and your teeth are all amazingly unique for you!

- You are unique.
- You add value.
- You are special.
- You are important.

Your genetic make-up, educational background, career, and family structure are a blessing. You have an experience like none other – no one can feel what you feel or love the way you love – you are indeed tailor-made! As women, we have been blessed with the spirit of resilience. We go through many changes in life from our adolescent years and on through our adult years – not to mention the many physical changes our bodies endure: teen acne, puberty, pregnancy, childbirth, menopause, post-menopause, and the lists go on. Each phase in your life is purposeful and intentional! I believe that yours, mine, "our" purpose in life is, first and foremost, to yield to the teaching of God through the Holy Spirit and to minister the gospel of Salvation. As we find salvation within ourselves, we are presented with key moments throughout our lives in which we are chosen to minister hope for healing because we can relate to the pain and therefore minister healing most effectively. Sweetheart, He chose you! Whether He met you in the darkness of a particular crossfire – as He did with me, or He met you in your glory serving – either way, He chose you.

Chapter 3:

The Pursuit of God...

My days are met with an aggressive pursuit to hear from God. Most days I find inspiration by listening to a sermon found on YouTube, a Podcast, or a CD that I am looking to as a resource to answer questions about an event that is happening in my life. I live in the Atlanta-metro area and for those who are familiar with the traffic – you will agree that any commute can be simultaneously precious and draining. I am grateful for the women who align their faith with mine on a regular basis, most particularly:

- Melanie Gaskins
- Alison Burden
- TDReid
- Sheryl Hines
- Trinise Preston, and
- Wanda Lewis – a dear friend who earned her wings in June 2019

I adore and respect this group of women who hold me accountable for being the best Cathy; they hold no judgment, and they are comfortable with doing what I call a "gut-check." We pray! We fast! We get angry! We fight in the spirit for the good of each other!

I believe in the death, burial, and resurrection of my Lord and Savior, Jesus Christ! I believe in the trinity – God the Father, God the Son and God the Holy Spirit. I believe that every area in my life has been pre-ordained by my Father. He sent specific instructions to His Son to include every adversity that I will face, and when my Savior stretched forth His hands to be nailed to the cross on Calvary – my pain and suffering were included along with my healing. Let's just stop for a minute and process that thought… For every issue that we face – it was pre-ordained before the earth was formed, and God loves us (present tense) so much that He gave (past tense) a command to His Son to absorb every battle of pain; by His stripes – we are healed according to Isaiah 53:5. All worry, care, pain, mental anguish, scars, images, bondage, slavery – any manner of pain and suffering, they were included… That's love! Jesus Christ is the epitome of obedience; He knew that in the physical, He would feel the pain set before Him as He prepared for His journey to Calvary – BUT HE LOVES US SO MUCH that He said "YES" to our Father. Luke 22:42 tells us, "Father, if it is

Your will, take this cup away from me: nevertheless, not My will, but Yours, be done" (NKJV).

Because Jesus was the Spirit of God in the form of man, He was able to comprehend what we would feel as human beings – nothing was off the table! Jesus felt – emotionally, physically, mentally and sociably. That's why when He died on the cross, the Holy Spirit took the next shift (so to speak); He is our helper (John 14:16).

Hebrews 4:12

"...for the Word of God is quick, and powerful, and sharper than any two-edge sword, piercing even to the dividing asunder of soul and spirit, and joints and marrow, and is a discerner of the thoughts and intents of the heart" (KJV).

I believe in the bible! It is alive, and it speaks to me; in fact, Psalm 50:7 instructs us to hear and God will speak! Psalm 107:20 tells us that "He sent his Word and healed them, and delivered them from their destructions." My friend, God's Word is alive! I have learned not to limit myself in the way that God speaks to me. there are times when I am awakened by the Holy Spirit who speaks to my heart and he offers a scripture. Other times, I am awakened, praying in my heavenly language. I've come to the revelation that God can only speak to me when I am willing to listen. You might be wondering, who is this chick

and why does she mention her "experiences" so much…?
Great question, angel-heart – let me tell you a little bit
about who I am.

Chapter 4:

I am Peculiar - For Good Reason...

I've been asked, "What are you?"

My reply is usually a sarcastic, "Human, how about you?" I know exactly what people are asking, but I also correct them when they assume.

I was recently at a doctor's appointment and the nurse confirmed my profile – when she got to my race, she cited "Caucasian."

I replied, "No ma'am, do you have a bi-racial category?"

She told me, "No."

I responded, "What categories do you have?"

She rambled off her list, to which I retorted, "Other."

I am what many people title as a "mixed" race; I snicker as I type the term, then default to thinking, "What on earth does mixed mean?" Well, my mother is a white woman who was born and raised in Waycross, Georgia. My father is a black man who was born and raised in Compton, California (I think – stick with me - I'll come back to my dad shortly). Today, interracial families are not uncommon – we still have a way to go before we cross the finish line to interracial acceptance; however, we are making progress! Dating and marrying outside of our race is more common today than it was when I was younger – whew, PRAISE GOD!

From this point forward - as you read – please be aware that inviting you into my childhood and painful events from my past opens the door to reveal dark sides about my parents; this is a part of my therapy and healing process and it is not intended to devalue my parents. It's important to know that I forgive them, and I am grateful to God for using them as the vessel through which the oil flowed to get me here. I am mature enough in scripture to know that the principalities used to operate in them were intentional for this moment in my life – yours too. You were a part of the plan; that's why you're reading this book! Satan was unaware of how God would use me to help other women. So – take that, Holy Spirit - Girl Power Punch. We win!

I was born Cathy Diane McDade on September 3, 1973 to James and Kathy McDade. I grew up on the Northside of Jacksonville, Florida in a home with two of my ten siblings. Princess is one year older and Jammie is five years younger than me. My mother gave birth to five girls – the first three have a different father. My father had five children from a previous marriage; my baby sister and I are from his second wife (Kathy). We were pretty much a well-kept secret. In fact, I remember my eldest brother, who is now with the Lord, telling me that when he met my mom – our father told him that she was his nurse.

Lies.

Lies.

Lies… My mother was never a nurse – the two were having an affair. Remember earlier, when I mentioned "dysfunctional?" My dear, you can now delete that term from your vocabulary – dysfunctional as identified by societal standards is normal.

My childhood was very violent - oh my God, it was very violent! I watched my father drink heavily and fight like a madman! His temper was out of control – he was a raging bull who had no compassion for his daughters. When I think about protection, James is not the first person who comes to mind. He was not seated at the head of the table during Sunday dinners, nor was he encouraging us to look for Easter eggs. He was not the umpire, referee, prayer warrior, chauffer, nor host during family game night. We did not pray together; there were no park visits, sports played nor recreational activities to help us enhance our socialization skills or team sportsmanship – there was not even an acknowledgment of our accomplishments that would forward the thought of advancing to another level -

not even the the earthly equivalent of "Well-done" daughter; I am so proud of you."

Most people that I talk with about their childhoods have good, solid, strong memories of holidays – mine are an absolute blur. Our family structure was very different than those of other families – especially those in our neighborhood. I'd venture to guest that my parents were married for about ten years. I remember that when I turned nine years old,my mom introduced my sisters and me to "Butch," whom she had a long-term relationship with. To this day I call him, "Pop." He was one of the best men that my mother ever interacted with. The value I learned from the timemy mom and Butch were together was this: it is never okay for a man to hit a woman. Butch married a woman named Susan. She has been accepting of my sisters and me since day one. In fact, our children call them G-ma and G-pa; they are our family – not by blood, but by love. Thank you, Pop and Susan for accepting us!

Chapter 5:

My Destructive Mom...

My family scars run deep - deeper than I care to research. In fact, I've been delivered from wanting to know any more because of the wounds that cover scarred tissue. I've resolved in my spirit that what I needed from my mother - yet did not receive - inspired me to provide for my two daughters.

Nurturing.

Hugs/kisses.

I love you's.

Tea/Coffee time.

Words of affirmation and encouragement.

I didn't know how much I needed those things from my mother until my early 30's. Memories of my mom are saturated with darkness. I am of the opinion that she was very unhappy with her childhood, and she replicated her mother, Faye. I met Faye for the first time when I was in my early 30's – it was at my cousin's wedding in Waycross, GA.

My mother introduced us, "Cathy, this is Faye. Faye, this is little Cathy."

I extended my hand to shake hers and said, "It's very nice to meet you, Faye."

She reciprocated, "It's nice to see you again."

I later asked my mom who Faye was.

She admitted, "she's my mother." I nearly burst with anger.

My first thought was, *where was she when I was a kid?* I never had the chance – never in life - to say "Grandmother, Grandfather, Aunt, Uncle – nothing…" Naturally, I wanted to give Faye a piece of my unholy-spirit-filled mind… About six months later, I saw Faye again. My cousin's husband was murdered, and I was old enough to provide support, so my daughters and I drove to Waycross. I asked Faye if I could call her – she obliged by giving me her phone number, an obligation which I sat on for a few weeks. I didn't know what to say or how to interact with her; furthermore, I was severely scarred and underdeveloped in my spiritual walk. Our first call went like this.

I started off, "Hello, Faye – how are you?"

Faye replied, "I am good, how are you?"

I responded, "I am good." I heard nothing but silence in return. "Faye, where were you when I was growing up?"

"I have to cook dinner," she dismissed.

"Goodbye," is the last thing I said to her.

Faye and I never spoke again. I simply chalked that conversation up to this: she missed out on getting to know a really cool chick, and I missed out on receiving the love that a grandmother has to give. Seeds of destruction were planted in that moment, but God had a better plan for filling my "grandparent" cup!

My mother was married when she met my dad, who was her senior by fourteen years. I speculate that she saw an opportunity to escape her life of bondage in Waycross with my dad. My mother gave birth to her first daughter as a teenager – I am not entirely sure, but I believe that she was either 14 or 15 at the time. When she met and married my dad, she had two daughters and she was pregnant with her third. I did not grow up with my sisters from my mom's previous marriage – in fact, I didn't meet them until I had my first child at the age of 14 (praise God - the generational curse of teenage pregnancy stopped with me). My mother was married to a white man before she met my dad, and as you could imagine, the mentality of whites in Waycross, Georgia in the '70s did not support a white woman taking her two white babies to be raised by a black man. Are you kidding?

I suspect it to have been a tough decision for my mom to hand over her children, but she did. My mother gave her daughters to their white father and she missed the opportunity to raise them. I'm sure there's more to the story. I knew my mother had sisters; however, my memory only recalls one - Annette who seemed to have been supportive of my mom (based on my observations). I am left to believe that neither of her other sisters had no interest in being an aunt to their mixed nieces. In fact, I recall a time when my mother's family came to our house in Jacksonville to get my sister Princess, while leaving Jammie and me (the mixed kids) behind.

Rejected

Unwanted....

Satan was very subtle in sifting me as wheat while he strategically planted the seed of not being wanted – it worked for many years. But God! Mom told me stories of how her white side of the family wanted to kill me because I was a "nigger baby" – can you believe that? I am literally shaking my head because I will never understand how a "loving mother" could part her lips and plant the seeds of being rejected by family in her daughter's head.

Nurture me, mother... Nurture me... I needed you...

The seed of being unwanted was watered regularly, and the feeling of abandonment began to form along with the self-images of:

- Self-doubt
- I am "less-than"
- I am not good enough
- I am unwanted
- I am unloved
- I am unchosen
- ...and, I am the hated "nigger baby" (my eyes well with tears as I type this; again, this is a healthy emotional release – this part of my life is over).

My sister Princess is a year older than I. I assume that my mom and dad were married at the time she was born, because she was given my dad's last name. He raised her as his own. As I reflect on our childhood years, I'd say that Princess suffered the worst – even to this day, her scars run deep.

Talking with her as a woman of God enables me to discern the spirits that haunt her - and they make themselves known during the conversation. She protects herself by being angry, cold, and callous – these are the masks she wears to avoid the responsibility of allowing anyone to penetrate her trust-barrier. She's been hurt! Princess was known as the white girl who wanted to be black. We'd hear people say that she talked black; acted black. I don't know what that really means, but she also dated black guys and eventually had bi-racial children. She gave birth to her first son at the age of 15 (generational curse). That Princess subscribed to the ways of the culture that she grew up in makes perfect sense – she grew up in a predominately black neighborhood. On top of that, she viewed my father as her natural dad, and the combination resulted in the influences of black culture being absorbed by her psyche. She, too, was rejected by her father, andeventually our mother - now she rejects people when they get close to her. It's no wonder she has barriers as deep as the ocean floor… Father God touch my sister right now and let the manifested power of Your healing begin to take root to utterly destroy the calcified roots that have plagued her with feelings of rejection, abandonment, anger, and bitterness - in the name of Jesus.

Jammie. She will always be "my little sister," no matter her age. She was a precious little baby – a little chunky baby… I remember when my mother bought her home from the hospital; she was so tiny, and she made these noises that I was unfamiliar with. She was so adorable. She had wild, jet-black, thick, curly hair. She had a gap in her little teeth, and she was so desperate to be loved on. She was the youngest and was the recipient of brutality – from James, Kathy, Princess, and me. You see, an abused child can suppress pain for a short amount of time; eventually, the abused will turn into the abuser.

That's what happened with my sisters and me – we began abusing each other, and my poor baby sister received the brunt of the abuse. Sad, but true… Child abuse turns into adolescent anger, period… It comes out in many ways:

- Self-mutilation.
- Substance and alcohol abuse.
- Promiscuity.
- Acts of violence towards others.

The old saying holds true that if you kick a dog, he might run away, but if you keep kicking him, he will retaliate – that's what we did as little girls. God, I repent for every time I hurt my siblings or any other child. I repent… Jammie was the pressure-valve: she was an outlet for anger to be released by Princess and me. We were a "fighting" family. I can't even use the term, "family" here – that's not what we were… We were a pack of wolves tearing each other to shreds, and it began with James and Kathy!

I watched my little sister develop into a carbon-copy of my father, which I found odd considering that my parents divorced when she was about five – how could she be so much like James? Like my mother, Princess, and me, Jammie was also a teenage mother – giving birth at 15 (Generational curses). She, too, suffered from an identity crisis – just like Princess, my mother and me. Jammie was married off at the age of 15, and she gave birth to three beautiful children. The sweet girl has been through hell and back many times in her life – only because of the seeds that were planted. I am happy to share that she has rededicated her life to Christ; she has sought counseling and has claimed healing, deliverance, and restoration over her life. Now that I understand the importance of nurturing – I am able to nurture my little sister through scripture and I align my faith with hers – she is well in every area of her life! Hallelujah!

I've often heard that every family has its fair-share of scandal – the McDade's were no different! Our family tree wreaks of the foul stench of secrecy, lies, deception, molestation, alcoholism, adultery, and hypocrisy! During my healing process, doors to lies have been opened, and yes, I have confronted many of them. I have concludde that the evil, hideous masks that James and Kathy handcrafted and wore as a result of their self-serving "lusts of the flesh" stand asdriving forces behind my deliberate intention to share "who I am" – especially with my children and grandchildren.

I was named after my mother, and I've been told that I look like her. However, as I age, I see both of my parent's features in me. Kathy was one of the most beautiful women that I'd ever seen. She looked like a thicker version of Linda Carter (the Original Wonder Woman). She had dark hair, blue eyes, high cheekbones – I mean, the lady was stunningly gorgeous! She had a nice figure - very curvaceous. She was a short little stallion - very sexy! Her make-up was always flawless! As a kid, I'd sit on the toilet seat and watch her get ready for work – she'd apply her makeup, hot curl her hair, use half-a-can of hair spray to hold it in place, and then when she was done, she'd take one last glance at herself in the mirror – she'd look at herself right in the eyes and say mean things to herself:

- ♣ "You're so fat".
- ♣ "You need a tan"
- ♣ "Your hair is a mess"
- ♣ "Your teeth are yellow."

Pause!

Chapter 6:

Identity Crisis Alert!

Kathy didn't see herself as the beautiful woman that I saw. Did she self-sabotage, destroying her own self-image? Was she able to identify with who she is in the body of Christ? Why did she own what others said about her – why did she own the negative thoughts of herself? Why did she devalue herself right there in my presence? The way Kathy viewed herself, the way she thought of herself, and the way she talked to herself is exactly what she taught her daughters...

Mommy nurture me – please...

My mother did not graduate from high school; she worked lower-paying jobs to make ends meet – at times, she worked two jobs after she and my dad divorced. As a mother, I not only relate with her, but I also empathize – you do what you have to do to take care of your children.

As a child, my description of my mother in one word is, "angry." Kathy was very beautiful, but extremely angry; she didn't smile or laugh. She didn't dance or exercise. She didn't have a girl's night out or socialize with many women. However, I do recall one friend, LeAnn. We would go to LeAnn's house to escape the abuse of my father, but we didn't stay long; my mother eventually found herself going right back to the circle - the circle of rage, abuse, and violence.

Kathy listened to sad love songs, cried a lot, and lashed out with rage on a regular basis. She worked standing on her feet. I remember massaging her feet as a kid to make her feel better; I tried to comfort her any way that I could. I have vague memories of Kathy cooking. I have no memories of picnics. There are a few memories of going to the beach (which became a way of life for my sisters, me and our children later in life). I don't remember having breakfast dates. We didn't take walks in the park. There were no ballet lessons, track meets, recitals, cheerleading practices, gym outings, or swim competitions. There was an abundance of open hand slaps in the face, closed fist punches, names being called, hair being pulled, and anger! Rage! There were deliberate attempts to destroy my sisters and me. In fact, my mother became so physically violent towards my sister, Princess, and me that she beat us with a plunger as if she were fighting off a would-be murderer – it was just that aggressive!

She marked us!

At about ten years old, I was called a bitch for the first time (that I can remember), and then I was called a whore. By whom? By Kathy... How damaging! If my mother's perspective of me was so degrading, where would I get the notion that anyone else would see me any differently? I grew in her stomach for nine months, and she labored for me... Or did she? I often ask myself why didn't she love me more? Why didn't she plant seeds of confidence and hope inside of me?

She scarred me.

She left me with the feeling that I was worthless, that I was dirt, and that no one wanted me. Where did her behaviors generate from? I suspect Kathy had thoughts of being alone with no support system – she could have been on an island by herself; after all, she was a white woman from Waycross, Georgia who married a black man who may have just sold her a pipe dream. She married him and she obviously trusted him with not only her life but also the lives of her children. He let her down. He probably broke her at her most vulnerable lowest point ever in life, and she probably never recovered from that. I also suspect that my mother followed in her mother's footsteps - another generation of women who aborted learning their identity in Christ:

Faye planted the seed with Kathy

Kathy planted the seed with her daughters...

❧ Mommy nurture me...

❧ My mother was my first heartbreak.

But God...

My mother left me when I was fifteen – she literally left me in an empty house. My observation of my mother is that she is a woman who spent her life trying to find happiness in people and tangible things. If you can give her money, she's your best friend. I remember my mom showing me a check for a thousand dollars that was written to her by her common-law husband, Grant. They never legally got married but they've lived in the same house for over 30 years now. When she showed me the check and said we are moving to Turtle Creek (which is a prominent area back then in Jacksonville), she was very excited about the house – it was a three-bedroom, two-bathroom house. It was big compared to where we were. It had a pool and gazebo in the backyard – a beautifully manicured yard. She was proud of her new home; it filled her cup:

I asked her, "Mom when are we moving?"

She replied, "Grant said that you and Princess cannot come, only Jammie."

I responded, "What do you mean we can't come?"

"Grant said that he doesn't want you all living with us."

"What are we going to do?"

"Well you guys can rent this house."

"Mom I'm 15 years old and actually, I'm still in school. We are minors; no one is going to agree to rent us a house."

Chapter 7:

Compassion To Move Forward

When I think about my childhood and what I experienced at the hands of my mother – the on-set is anger... I never let it last for too long though; if I stay in the dark place of negative reflection, then I abort the development process of walking in the light, and I am ultimately led to a strong feeling of compassion towards my mother. It is my prayer that she will yield to God, giving him an opportunity to fill her with his presence and offer her the peace that only He can give.

Psalm 139: 7-8

"Where can I go from Your Spirit? Or where can I flee from Your presence? If I ascend into heaven, You are there; If I make my bed in hell, behold, You are there"
(NKJV).

There are times when I get emotional – I lived a carbon-copy of my mother's life. I was arrested by the Holy Spirit and by God's grace. I willingly opened my heart, Lord I welcome you! Your presence is so powerful. It is by your mercy that, on the other side of each challenging scenario, I still come out on the back-end smiling. You are always here despite the situation. Sometimes I don't understand it, but you do, so who am I to say, "No, take this situation away, Lord?"

I am guilty, at times, of trying too hard to influence others to tap into scripture. I am a teacher, and when I get the "ah-ha" moments, I immediately want to share them. Sometimes I have to take a step back, because others may not be ready. There were certain times I'd invite my mom into scripture, or I'd send her YouTube videos via iPhone text. Other times I would call her and say, "Hey, just wanted to see how you are doing." One day, by faith, we will be able to sit down and have a cup of tea together – we will be able to talk as two women who fought hard as mothers. As an adult, today, I subscribe to the opinion that we can't change the past. What we can do is recognize that this is where we are. If I were speaking directly to my mother, I'd encourage her to look into the mirror. The circumstances that she's endured and the circles of influences that have surrounded her are the factors that have influenced the way I see, feel, respond, and act - whether my actions are right or wrong. As women - as human beings - whenever we can stop to say, "I love you enough to sacrifice myself for your happiness," and it comes from a place where the Holy Spirit dwells, we can rest in knowing that God is here..

Who am I to judge? I mean, really.... Who am I? Christ died on Calvary for all of us. Voluntarily and lovingly, He stretched out his arms, knowing that it was going to hurt - talk about love. Like 23:34 tells us that Jesus said, "Father, forgive them, for they do not know what they do." He said this even as they divided His garments and cast lots... He took a crown of thorns because he loved us! Christ absorbed all of our pain, all of our discomfort, all of our turmoil, all of our depression, and all of our abuse – He took it all! When He did, His cleansing blood offered me the opportunity to "let go" and move forward with compassion!

- The blood.
- The blood.
- The blood of Jesus was shed for us.
- We have been redeemed from the curses of the world.
- Now, there is a choice.
- It is your choice to accept the redemption of Christ.

The compassion that I have for you, Mom, runs deeper than our scars. I encourage you to tap into the presence, the power, and the anointing of the Holy Spirit - let God change you dramatically. I can share from experience - when I take a step back and I look at some of the mistakes that I made as a mom, I understand that I replicated what I saw. As soon as I recognized that my actions were damaging my own daughters, I had to make a choice to correct the behavior – it wasn't easy! If I didn't change, the cycle would have continue, and my girls would have done what Faye did – three generations earlier. It stops with me!

Chapter 8:

I Forgive You, Mom

Parenting is a rough journey – no matter how many books we read, it's a rough ride…. Mom, I forgive you. I trust in God that one day the Holy Spirit will rest on your soul, that he will meet you where you are and heal you so that you never have to feel the pain again. Whatever it is that has kept you in bondage – let it go! Be free so that you can help someone else. You are not alone, and you are not the only woman who's experienced pain at the hands of a man. You have been redeemed by the blood of the cross, and you can walk in your healing right now – today if you want to.

- ❧ I forgive you, Kathy Diane McDade
- ❧ Oh my God, I forgive you…
- ❧ I love you with Christ-like love.

The women from your womb are blessed! From me to my daughters, to my granddaughters – the fruit of your womb is blessed! Mother, I love you enough to let you know that no matter what you've experienced – it's over… If you need someone to blame, then I'll take the blame so that you can be healed. I trust in God that, one day, you will want to know me as your daughter - as an adult. I harbor no bitterness noranger towards you – you are worthof forgiveness. I forgive you so that we are not destroyed anymore; may the blessing of the Lord, God Almighty rest upon us both - now and forevermore. May you walk in your healing and in the Spirit of Forgiveness. In the name of Jesus, Amen.

Chapter 9:

My Destructive Dad...

Profane language. Rage. Anger. Alcoholism. Adultery. Domestic and child abuse.

My father James was my first example of what to look for in a man. My thoughts of him are engulfed with brutality... Daddy, why didn't you protect me?

I remember one particular fight between him and my mom: they were in the kitchen, he had his hands around her throat, she was bent over the stove, and I

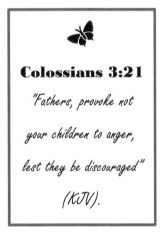

Colossians 3:21

"Fathers, provoke not your children to anger, lest they be discouraged"

(KJV).

remember propping myself up between the table and chair. I was screaming with tears and fear – stop, stop, please stop! Gosh, I am tearing up as that memory resurrects itself as an image in my head... Father, thank you for healing me! The police were notified many times of the acts of domestic violence against my mother, but she always went back to him. I believe wholeheartedly that my dad was simply a broken man who aspired to live "the good life," according to worldly standards. From as far back as I can remember, he would over-embellished details about his life. For example, he claims that he had twenty-two children and that he was a fighter pilot in the Navy. The facts: James molested my sister Princess while he was married to my mother, he molested me when I was fifteen, he made sexual advances towards me as as of May, 2019 (which is when I cut my ties with him), and he made advances towards my baby sister in 2015. He is demonically-influenced and will have to give an account for the gifts that God entrusted in his hands. His shackles are in the form of women, alcohol, lies, manipulation, and deception. He is in bondage for sure...

James served in the US Navy – as a kid, I remember him being very tall and intimidating. He had a deep voice - almost thunderous! He spoke with demand and authority. He lacked patience and he never praised his daughters. He was 6'1, and I was this itty-bitty kid who would look up at what seemed to be a giant man. He'd get angry when I didn't understand math and he would spank me because I'd get a math problem wrong. His spankings were humiliating, degrading, and damaging – he'd make my sisters and me pull our pants down, and he'd hit us with either his bare hand or a leather belt. It was so painful! It seemed like spankings would last forever. When they were over, I'd run to my room, hide in my closet, and cry until there were no more tears to flow. James marked me by breaking me.

- Daddy, protect me…
- My father was my second heartbreak.

James's military uniform was impressive - it was white and nicely decorated with badges of honor that he earned while serving his country. He looked so handsome and so distinguished. He was such a good-looking man. I remember that when he picked us up from school in his uniform one day, he turned the heads of the teachers. He moved with confidence and swag as we followed behind him like little ducklings. He always smelled good; he was nicely groomed,cleanly shaven, and he maintained the appearance of a well-kept man - very meticulously dressed… He was articulate - he spoke very proper English. He was impressive - to those he preyed upon…

James (my dad) was a manipulator. A liar. A con artist. An adulterous man. He told folks that he flew planes during his Navy career; in reality,he was a chef.

A chef!

As I got older, I wondered, *why would this man be dishonest about his career in the military?* During his era, being a part of a government entity was an accomplishment in and of itself; I cannot understand why he did not appreciate who he was at that moment and embrace the life that he lived while serving his country. I would have more respect for him had he just said something along the lines of, "You know what - when I joined the military my desire was to be a pilot, but I ended up becoming a chef. It doesn't matter, though, because now I'm getting a retirement check, and I served my Country - my military career didn't pan out the way I expected, but my life is a blessing." His lack of integrity influences my level of recognition for who he is in my life; thus, I identify him by his first name for the most part, instead of referring to him as, "Dad." There are different components of his life that he was very dishonest about. However, before my eldest brother passed away in 2016 from cancer, he shared a lot with me about our father – he included a time in which he defended himself against my dad because he was tired of suffering at the hand of his abuse.

On a positive note, James rented space along a small strip-plaza - a storefront piece of property on Soutel Drive in Jacksonville. His aspiration for entrepreneurship led him to open McDade's Thrift Store – his niche' was in fixing appliances. He was very crafty with his hands; he was an all-around fix-it kind of guy. I spent a lot of time playing under the display cabinet at the thrift store and came to know the customers – especially the women.

What follows is my introduction to "adultery" – the seed was planted… James and Brenda… I'll never forget her. She was dark in complexion and beautiful - very curvy. I remember being at the store with my dad one day, and playing in my usual spot – under the display counter… I emerged and walked to the back of the store only to find my dad between Brenda's legs; kissing her. I may have been about seven or eight years old - as a kid, what do you say?

"Whoa. Wait!"

Now what?

"MOM!!!!!!" Yep, you guessed it! I told my mother…
"Mom, I saw dad and Ms. Brenda kissing."
I met the crossfire between integrity and fear!

My father told me to tell my mother I was lying about him.

My mother told me to tell her what I saw.

I was in a state of confusion.

Oh my God. What was I supposed to do? It was so unfair to be in that kind of position. James always said, "If you tell me the truth, I will be able to defend you; but, if you lie to me once, I'll never be able to trust you again." Really, that's his quote…

On another occasion, I witnessed my dad flirting with our neighbor, Jackie – her husband was Mike. Jackie was also very beautiful - she had this reddish-brown Afro and a very beautiful complexion. She, too, is very curvaceous! Jackie and my mom got into a physical fight in the parking lot of the corner store. I could not fathom why two women were outside in broad daylight, fighting on the parking lot. Based on what I know about James McDade today, I comfortably speculate that my mom may have confronted Jackie about having an affair with my dad. Ultimately, Mike and Jackie moved away - when a new family moved in next door, my parents were separated.

James had a gift for handyman work – he could tear apart a radio, pour concrete, tile a roof, and lay tile. He could build or fix just about anything! He took pride in our home – in fact, he built extra space to expand upon our living space. Our house was very small, but I thought it was huge! He built two mirrored bars, which is probably why I have a fascination for mirrored bar areas. If you came to our house, then after getting past the front door that had an aluminum makeshift cover over the opening where the glass used to be and was broken out by my dad, you'd come into the small entryway. There, you'd be greeted by a reflection of your appearance - an array of mirrors. Stepping down into the den on the left – and off to the right - you'd find cabinets under his bar. I was so small at that time that I would crawl inside the cabinets and pretend they were my house. James built the bar and den area by hand – he poured the concrete; knocked out the back walls and installed double-doors which led to the back yard. Every now and again, I have dreams about that house - I'm not sure why.

We attended church on a regular basis - in fact, James kept a stash of peppermint balls in his pockets to mask the smell of liquor on his breath, but it didn't work. He enjoyed singing along with the choir, but as soon as we left the church – we went back to a life of chaos. My sisters and I dressed alike, and we had to present ourselves as little soldiers – we were not to embarrass him, or there would be a consequence to pay. The abuse from my parents became expected. Normal. James would start drinking, he and Kathy would begin fighting, my sisters and I would fight next, and then we'd get a spanking. I was filled with that same rage that my parents had – they passed it down to me. I would find bricks and literally throw them at the mirrors in the house, shattering them into pieces. At the time, I had no concept of why. Today, I am fully aware that I was replicating what I saw. James was notorious for destroying furniture when he drank! He'd break the coffee and end tables that were in the shape of angels. He would strategically glue them back together, only for them to be broken again from the acts of violent rages between my parents. Mirrors surrounded our home, yet they were broken - the house was dark and quiet unless my parents were fighting. I remember, once, trying to brush my hair while looking into one of the broken mirrors. As I struggled to tame my wild hair, my father continued to call me "ugly." James broke things – he broke his children and we were becoming just like him… His destructive seeds began to harvest…

Kids will repeat what they see…

I picked up a stray cat one day, and without knowing the responsibility of caring for an animal, I brought it home to claim it as my own. I would pick the cat up by the neck, and I would throw the cat down on the bed. I would hit the cat in the face. His little claws tried to secure themselves in my skin as he scratched me over and over again, but his efforts were futile - I didn't even care about the scratches. I was demonstrating the kind of anger that I witnessed from my parents, and I was too young to realize that it was wrong. Poor cat. Sometimes, I shake my head in shame at the thought of that period in my life. I developed an affinity for collecting reptiles – they had a purpose in my life. I would collect lizards, grasshoppers, and other "bugs" that I would save in empty jars lined up in my window. In my twisted attempt to care for them, I would collect grass and worms so that they were comfortable and fed well. I later wanted to see what their anatomy was like, so I began to dissect them. Praise God for deliverance, I would vomit at doing that today!

We had what seemed to be a huge back yard and a ditch that my sisters and I played in as often as we could.

We built tree houses, played kickball, and lived as what we knew to be the life of a child – that was our escape - because my father was out of control. We had a small social circle made up of kids in our neighborhood. We were not as accepted as other kids, or at least that's what I thought. It may have been the seeds of insecurity planted in me by my parents speaking. I am not sure whether the parents from other neighboring homes didn't see the violent behavior that my dad demonstrated, or whether life in the South during the 70's as a biracial kid just meant – tag, you're hated today. Either way, my days were filled with physical confrontation. Whether it was physical confrontation with kids from school or with my sisters, we would fight like nobody business - I mean scratches, bite marks, pulling each other's hair out as if we were just alley cats. We had no concept of a healthy lifestyle.

My elementary and Jr. High years were a strugglefilled with distractions from my home life; I was unable to focus, and I was tired a lot. I was also the kid with crooked teeth. My two front teeth were jacked up! Sometimes, I would take chewing gum, roll it into a ball, and fill in the gap where my tooth was pushed back. Then I would smile, which is something that I didn't do much of because of the shame I felt from my appearance – my teeth were horrid! I was a mixed girl with crazy hair and crooked teeth.

Elementary school was just as painful – kids were cruel - they'd call me hateful names like zebra, Oreo, black-white girl, confused, and mixed. Every degrading interracial name that you can think of, I was called that - not only by kids in the neighborhood, but by James as well. He had his fair share of calling my sisters and me degrading names like stupid, ugly, and ignorant.

There was one family that lived in the house on the corner - the father was a Pastor. I am grateful to him, his wife, and his sister for transporting my sisters and me to and from church on a regular basis. Pastor and his wife had five children – three boys and two girls. Lucky for us (my sisters and I), we got along; they were the most influential family. Getting to know them on a spiritual level was the beginning of my journey; I didn't know it at the time, however. Pastor Terry Hill Sr. would come to our house and pick us up in the church bus; he was the open vessel where the anointing oil began to flow – it was through him that I received the gift of speaking in the tongues and with the power of the Holy Spirit (I was nine when I was anointed, but it took years for my development). It was my new beginning. Jeremiah 29:11 tells me that God has a plan and a purpose for my life. The shift began with the influence of Pastor Hill and his family, people who demonstrated true family values – none like I knew at that time in my life.

Thank you, Pastor Hill!

Other kids in the neighborhood were not so friendly – they were very mean. They probably thought the same of us as well. One of my painful and perplexing memories is that of a little boy who threw a rock at me as I rode my bicycle around the circle. He hit my ankle, and it took a while to heal. To this day, I cannot understand why he did that. I forgive him, however... My life was patterned after so much hatred; my defense skills were tapped into at an early age because children in our neighborhood were constantly starting fights with my sisters and me! We started a few as well... I acted out angrily while in school for two reasons: fist, I was being abused at home, and second, I was being bullied at school. We were in fights every day – either before or after school with girls and boys. Yes, boys! Why would a boy want to fight a girl? I will never be able to answer that question... But it was true!

Helston Court had some good days – we called it "the Circle." It was literally that – a circle! I loved roller-skating and I tried to do it as much as I could! The best part about roller-skating in the circle was coming down the hill at a rapid pace and having to navigate successfully. There were a few girls in the neighborhood who were considered to be a positive circle of influence, two of them being Betty and Tiffany. They were my skating buddies! We'd skate on the pavement of the circle that we lived in –

and that became my safe zone. I escaped life by tapping into something that my body could do differently; instead of fighting all the time, I figured out different ways to roller-skate. That became my hobby... I spent a lot of time at Betty and Tiffany's house – they had several cousins - one one of them had a crush on me. I do not recall playing with this particular little boy - maybe that's a memory that I chose to erase. However, the one memory I have that stands out involving this kid is the instance when I was about 10 years old being hit for the very first time in the face with a closed fist by a boy. That was the first time a male other than my dad had ever hit me – that was the second stage of my acceptance ofbeing domestically abused by a man. I stood in front of him - unmoved. I was torn inside, but he never saw it. Betty said" oh my God!" as she covered her mouth in disbelief. I stood firmly; defiantly in front of the boy as if to make a statement – that didn't hurt me, you didn't hurt at all.

He hit me, again.

An in a robotic manner, I walked away as if I accepted his abuse.

Why?

I do not have an answer right now...

I do not remember many smiles as a child – I remember mostly days of crying and sad moments. I remember being called very foul names by the children in our neighborhood – it was hard growing up. I would tear apart campaign sign sticks and carry them as a form of protection because I was tired of being bullied. I was tired of being jumped on by other kids and feeling defeated. I would say, *you know - if anyone is going to fight me today, I'm going to hit them with a stick and hit them with a brick.* My way of releasing anger was byhurting someone or something, like an animal, and that person or animal that I wanted to hurt had nothing, absolutely nothing to do with the pain that I felt inside. That pain came from the harvested seeds that my parents had sown into my life.

Chapter 10:

Teenage Violations

 Philippians 2:1-4

"...if there is any consolation in Christ, if any comfort of love, if any fellowship in the Spirit; if any affection and mercy, fulfill my joy by being like-minded, having the same love, being of one accord, of one mind. Let nothing be done through selfish ambition or conceit, but in lowliness of mind let each esteem others better than himself. Let each of you look out not only for his own interests, but also for the interests of others" (NKJV).

In this section, I am inviting you into a few graphic details of my early teenage years. This is when "it gets real," as the young folks say... Parents, in this section, I implore you – with all respect intended - to perform a self-analysis of how you are parenting. I believe in disciplining children. However, when you spank out of anger and rage, you've crossed the line into abuse! Please get professional help – for the sake of healing both you and your child...

The little girl inside me cries out:

Mommy, nurture me:

- Hug me
- Kiss me
- Love on me
- Have tea time with me
- Talk with me, not to me
- Be patient with me – I am still learning
- Remember, you were once my age – today, it is harder...
- Show me how to be a woman...

Daddy, protect me:

- Cover me in prayer
- Lead by positive example
- Take me to a movie
- Hug me
- Tell me you love me
- Show me you love me
- Sacrifice for me
- Be my first date, show me what to be aware of in a man
- Please do not hit me...

I had to ask and answer the question, "Cathy, do you want to accept the responsibility of being healed?" My answer was, "Yes." Back in the 80's, Rick James had a song titled, "She was 17." I was only 13.

Shattered.

Violated.

Broken.

I attempted suicide for the first time at 13 (the second attempt was when I was fifteen). I fought off a would-be rapist, I lost my virginity to someone four years older than me, and I became pregnant – yes, at thirteen.

Chapter 11:

1ˢᵗ Attempted Suicide

My parents were divorced for a few years when I turned thirteen; in fact, Butch and Kathy had been together for a while, and we moved away from the circle into another house on 63ʳᵈ street. It was a more modern house – much nicer than the house that we lived in on Helston Court. We had a fresh start – a new house and a little relief from our drama-filled life! Princess and I attended Kirby Smith Jr. High School. On our first day there, we were met with the drama and we had to quickly let it be known that we were not going to tolerate being bullied. We were respected as the newcomers, but we were also provoked to fight. During my first year at Kirby, I was sent to a disciplinary school for hitting a girl in the face with a stapler – the school was Darnell Smith, and it was a combination of students who were there for disciplinary reasons; the other student population was made up of teenage mothers. Mr. Lumpkin was the presiding President at that time, and he clearly told me, "Cathy, I never want to see you here again."

I replied, "Yes, sir."

Adjusting to the new environment took its toll on all of us – Kathy, Butch, Princess, Jammie, and me. Kathy became more aggressive – angrier - and the abuse got worse. She would literally fight Princess and me like we were women in the street. I am not sure if we ever really respected her. Maybe we feared her, but even that had an expiration date… One day, when my mom was angry about something, she came into the room and attacked me – I mean literally pulled my hair and hit me in my face with a closed fist. At thirteen, I retaliated. I was at my breaking point. I fought my mother as if she was some random chick on the street; I scared myself at the outcome! I ran away from home for the first time, and ended up at my friends' house (Tip and Rena). I stepped into a new chapter of my life, where the level of defense was out of control. I later returned to my mom's house because I had to go back to school. I slumped into a depression, and one day I took a bottle of pain pills hoping to die. Obviously I did not take enough, because I am still here to write about it. I went to sleep. When I woke up, I felt so empty and broken inside. My mother attempted to admit me to Charter by the Sea, claiming that I was manic. Really, Kathy? Where did my behavior come from? You see, this is where I recruit the comfort of the Holy Spirit for peace; had she been a little more patient with her daughters, things would have been different. Yes - it angers me at times, but I have to step

58

back and pray… She did the same thing with my little sister, Jammie – she tried to admit her into a hospital. It got to a point where neither of her daughters showed any form of respect. Why didn't we? Would you guess?

You guessed right…

Learned behavior!

Chapter 12:

Attempted Rape

Kevin… Kevin was his name. If I saw him today, I would not know him – it all happened so fast. Butch was the eldest of seven kids. His mother was Mama Lou, and their family became our family. Butch's youngest sister and I were the same age, so we became good friends. I craved a family environment so much that I followed her around a lot. Well - she told me about a sexual encounter that she had with a guy named Kevin, so I assumed they were dating. I didn't ask; neither did she offer any information. One day after church, she, another neighborhood friend, and I went to Kevin's house together. We were still wearing our church clothes. We were all sitting in the living room, talking. Out of nowhere, Kevin jumped up, pulled me by my arm, and drug me to his room. I resisted to the best of my ability. I was screaming, "What are you doing?" All the while, I was trying to process what was going on… Was this really happening to me? Was this guy going to violate my body and rob me of my virginity? Not like this… God, no, please…

He threw me on his bed like a rag doll and laid his heavy body atop mine. I wiggled and squirmed while screaming for the girls upfront to help me, but they never came into the room. Why not? I wonder... Kevin pulled my dress up, tore my underwear, and held me down. He tried really hard to penetrate me, but I kept wiggling, so he wasn't able to have his way. It lasted for what seemed to be hours, and I begged for him to stop. I cried - please stop. Don't do this, don't do this. He eventually ejaculated on my stomach, and the smell was awful; afterward, he got up. I immediately jumped up and ran out of the house. My hair was messed up. My dress was messed up - I think it may have been torn, I don't know One thing I do know is that I never saw that dress again. I did not even stop to get my underwear or my shoes. I ran. It has taken thirty-three years to open up about what Kevin did to me. I've never talked about it, I simply compartmentalized it – it was one of the most degrading moments in my life. During that same timeframe, a family friend visited came to my mom's house – he was an adult. I remember him putting his hand under my shirt, and rubbing my back when I sat next to him. The discomfort forced me to get up and go outside, only to have been awakened in the middle of the night with his fingers fondling my vagina. I told my mom about it, but nothing was done – the guy continued to come around... I still know him to this day, and out of respect for his wife, I refrain from disclosing his name... But, God knows, and he will give an account – I pray that he sought forgiveness...

Chapter 13:

Pregnant at 13

Ready for the World. My Melvin Riley look-alike…
My first crush. My first long-term boyfriend, and the father
of my two daughters, Darreial and DeJasma. Darrell is four
years my senior; today it's not a big deal, but he was
seventeen when we met. I was thirteen. He was more
experienced with dating - he was sexually active, and he
was my first everything. We had a ten-year stint of puppy
love, cohabitating, breaking up, getting back together, and
a love-hate relationship, but we severed ties - never to
reconcile our differences - when I was twenty-three.

I met Darrell through his cousin; we seem to have
clicked initially. He seemed innocent with a great sense of
humor. He was an only child. He and his mother Barbara
lived with his grandmother, whom he called "Mary."
Barbara was (and still is) a blessing – she is my children's
granny. I was thirteen when I became pregnant. Imagine
that… I was still battling with the demons of childhood
abuse – I was so green! Oblivious. But one thing was for
sure – Darrell gave me what I wanted from James and
Kathy. He hugged me, kissed me, and accepted me – with

my frazzled wild hair, crooked teeth, freckles, and, above all, my life as a bi-racial person.

- 🐾 Pause.
- 🐾 Parents, let me help you… Your daughters will look for what they want from you naturally. Something or someone will fill that void, so wise up - and give them as much of you as you can in the healthiest manner possible. If you miss this mark, it's a hard road to recovery.

I was very embarrassed when I returned to Darnell Cookman. The look on Mr. Lumpkin's face was gut-wrenching – that was the first time in my life that I felt like I disappointed anyone. He cared about my future, and when I returned to his school as a pregnant teen, I violated our agreement. I was able to redeem myself with Mr. Lumpkin – he proofed my undergrad thesis, and we were able to talk about my teenage pregnancy. Barbara didn't know that I was pregnant - she found out the day that I was released from the hospital, after giving birth to Darreial. I was fourteen and Darrell soon turned eighteen. Oh, God!

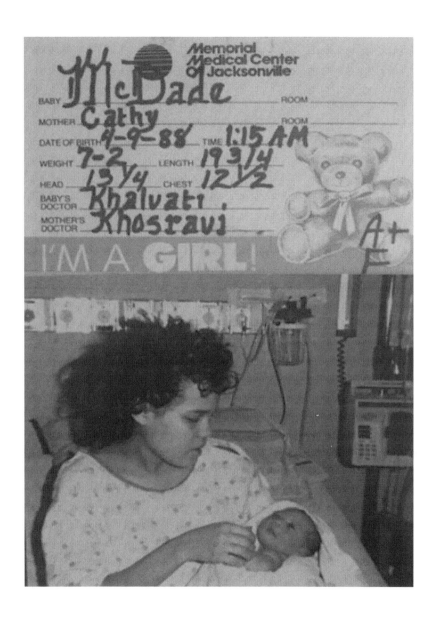

Darreial Chaunelle Miller was born on April 9, 1988. I looked at this little person with amazement. WOW – she came out of me... I was too young to process how her cells were developed, the cycle of procreation, or what my body experienced. In fact, I remember her first soiled diaper – I told Darrell that it was tar...

TAR!

How does a human being pass tar...?

God bless your Holy name...

I shake my head as I type....

I was young, and I had a lot to learn... Darreial had needs – she was a growing baby, and with me being fourteen, I wasn't able to work or provide for her financially. I depended on government assistance and help from my mom. Darrell did not complete high school; however, he had a job at a fast-food restaurant, and he provided for Darreial when he could. I did not have enough experience to expect more help from him than he provided – his support was a support of convenience, meaning he did for Darreial when he wanted to. Darrell and I began having relationship problems soon after Darreial was born – we'd break up to make-up, and it became a repetitive cycle of on-again, off-again nonsense.

My mom, Butch, Princess, Jammie – now, Darreial and I moved a few times more, eventually landing in a small shotgun house. I understand the pressure that my mom had – now, four children to provide for. Butch and Kathy broke up when I was fifteen. He later told me that he caught her with another man, Grant. She told Butch that Grant was Jammie's father, which is why she was with him during the time Butch saw them together. He was torn... I did not see Butch again for a few years, and I never knew why he just left until I was in my 30's. He protected my mother's dignity – even after she cheated on him.

Earlier, I shared with you that my mom left me when I was fifteen. Darreial and I were homeless, with nowhere to go. Darrell and I moved in together with his mother, Barbara. I am grateful that she took us in! Darrell became a different person. He turned into Nino Brown from the movie New Jack City - or he tried to, at least... Through him, I was introduced to crack cocaine. I wasn't a user – praise God - but I was tempted... For the sake of his dignity – I'll leave it at that. Darrell became abusive – verbally and physically. He would slap me, push me, punch me, and cuss me out like I was Alabama trash. We would fight everyday, it seemed like. We were young. We both suffered from a lack of parental guidance, and the pressures of life began to challenge us in ways where we had no experience or knowledge of resources to tap into.

Having a child, as a child, was super crazy! Darrell and I were trying our best to figure it out. I eventually dropped out of school and started a job at a fast-food restaurant to try and help financially. I began working at fifteen because I owned the responsibility of feeding my baby. I would walk to and from work. One particular day, when Darrell's mom was at work, I came home after working my shift – he was upset, and the worst fight that we'd ever had ensued. I remember him hitting me so hard that I fell on the floor of the duplex apartment that we lived in – he kicked me in my stomach and left me there laying like a dog. I felt so hopeless. Ashamed. Worthless. I laid there crying, unable to gather my thoughts about why this was happening. Then, my sister Princess called the house. Darrell answered the phone and yelled at me to take her call. I was so broken when I got to the phone that I couldn't really talk, but she was perceptive enough to know that something was wrong. She asked me, "Cathy what's wrong?" I could not get the words out...

She said to me, "Do you want me to call the police?"

I said, "Yes."

Sure enough, she called the police; that night, Darrell was arrested for domestic violence.

> Darrell - my children's father - was my third heartbreak.

Chapter 14:

2nd Attempted Suicide

Barbara knew about the drugs, but she kept quiet; she knew about the abuse, but she didn't intervene. When her son was arrested, she blamed me. Later that night – in the most awkward way - I put Darreial in her crib, got Darrell's gun, and went into the bathroom. I put the gun up to my head, and I pulled the trigger.

Nothing came out.

I pointed the gun at the floor.

It fired.

The bullet was stuck in the chamber, somehow, and when I pointed it away from me, it launched – it ricocheted from the floor to the ceiling, but it never hit me. I was so depressed because I wanted to die at that very moment, and I fell to the floor asking God, "Why am I still here?" Kathy came to Barbara's house that night and I told her, "Mom, he beat me up." She took Darreial and me to my dad's house that night. We went from bad to worse.

Chapter 15:

Molested by James

James was a filthy drunk and sick man – his demons must always have a field day with him! I have been released from the dark clichés of his sick, twisted perversion. Yet, when memories attempt to take me captive, I have to cast them down. Like right now, for example… Holy Spirit, help!

Darreial and I walked into James's house where the smell of kerosene and alcohol saturated his one-bedroom shack on the Eastside of Jacksonville, Odessa Street. He had so many women in and out of his house – it was pathetic! Drinking clouded his judgment. One particular night, I woke up to him massaging my breasts and fondling me while my baby was laying right next to me. I felt like I'd been drugged. When I woke up, I questioned if I was dreaming or if it in had, in fact, happened. It did. Later, he outright told me, "Cathy, I want to go to bed with you."

I replied, "I am your daughter, how could you say that to me?"

His reply was, "Fathers having sex with their daughters is in the bible." I was afraid, and I slept with a knife under my pillow until Darreial and I were able to leave.

Chapter 16:

Reunited with Darrell

After being separated for a while, Darrell and I reconciled our differences. He was my escape from James's house, but I didn't know which was worse – molestation from James or domestic violence from Darrell. We eventually got an apartment together - we kind of morphed into a couple, accepting each other's differences and trying to get along as friends. The truth is, however, that we were simply way too young, and we lacked the right sphere of influence to turn things around for the better. Drugs were a huge part of our lives – so was depression and violence. I began drinking alcohol, and it became my coping-substance of choice. There was one instance when I woke up looking at the barrel of a gun in my face with Darrell on the other end.

I was not afraid.

I had nothing to fight for.

I was just drained.

It was more of a scare tactic than anything. But he would always threaten me and say things like, no one can love you the way I do. You are not going to find anybody else like me. He started planting those seeds of insecurity. He would tell me that he was the best thing that ever happened to me, and yet we would still have these physical fights where the bruises, black eyes, and busted lips were the norms. Each fight got progressively worse! We repeated the same life that James and Kathy lived – another generational curse! Darrell was arrested several times for domestic violence, but we still ended up coming back together and nurturing the dysfunctional chaos of that hell-ationship (it wasn't a relationship – it was hell). At eighteen, after two abortions and one ectopic pregnancy, I became pregnant again. I had my second daughter De'Jasma "Jazz" on her dad's birthday, April 15, 1992 – I was nineteen. She was my little angel!

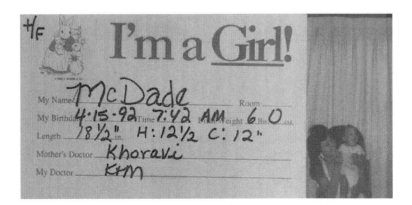

Chapter 17:

Darreial and Jazz

This chapter is dedicated specifically to my daughters - it is crafted as if I am speaking to them directly…

My beautiful daughters, you are the most precious people – not only do I love you dearly, but I also respect you and adore the women that you've become! I am so grateful to God Almighty - He who trusted me with you! I wasn't aware of the task at hand because I was a child when I became a mom. I did not know the severity of the responsibility of raising either of you – much less did I know how to be a woman for you to model after… Through you, God revealed His presence in many ways. He is real, and His plans for our lives is greater than we can imagine. Girls, WE WIN! There are details outlined in this material that you were not aware of. My decision to disclose certain details about James, Kathy, and your father are not intended to bring shame, but to open the door for the right healing – not only for me, but also for other women who are trapped in the bubble of being alone. Maintain your hunger and thirst after righteous living! When it gets hard, just know that you have a prayer partner in me, your mother!

Part 2:

Grafting A

New Character

Chapter 18:

Marriage

I am a woman who accepted lower standards in prior relationships because of my past, and because I didn't come into the full knowledge of where my pain came from. I didn't put the blame on the right person – I didn't even know there was blame to place until my early 40's. Luke 22:31 tells me that Satan asked for Simon Peter – he desired to, "…sift him as wheat." WHAT! What makes me any different? My response to Satan's attempt to sift me makes me different. As I began to take on a new character, I desired to be married and have a healthy life with someone. I was afraid, however, because I didn't want my anger to destroy my marriage. Here's one of my many conversations with God about being married – true story. This particular prayer may have occured in 1996'ish or so.

> "Dear God, hi – it's me, Cathy! God, I am so tired of being alone. I want a husband, can you bless me with one? The end and Amen."

Ha ha – where is the LOL emoji when I need it? Keep reading, Beloved.

I am of the mindset that, as adults, we still possess childlike tendencies – in many ways. That is not necessarily a bad thing. There's just something about the kid in us that naturally comes out at the right times - or, not… In my mid-forties, I still get excited about Disney movies! Although I am of the opinion that Walt Disney led many little girls to believe in fairytales that, in turn, gave them false hope, I nonetheless appreciate his creative imagination. One of my favorite Disney movies is Beauty and the Beast (1991). I remember watching it for the first time with my eldest daughter Darreial, who was three years old when the movie was released. To this day, I could watch that movie every weekend – when I do, the little girl in me curls up on the sofa with a throw blanket as I absorb all the romantic scenes.

The characters: Belle, her suiter Gaston, her father Maurice (who was overprotective as a result of the loss of his wife, and who worked as an inventor in their French village), and the Beast! Ahh, yes, the Beast - the Beast who was a prince by birth and was cursed by a mysterious Enchantress as punishment for his selfish and cruel nature The curse could only be broken if he could learn to love a woman and earn her love in return – only then could he receive freedom for himself and for those in the castle who were also affected by the spell, all because he could not love. He was given until his twenty-first birthday to reverse the curse. Each year leading up to his birthday, a pedal would fall from a rose that was given to him by the

Enchantress. It was the attraction to the rose that drew Maurice to the attention of the Beast. You see, Maurice's daughter Belle was his pride and joy, and she requested a single rose from him upon his return from a journey. I, too, love roses, but what lady doesn't, right?

Maurice met the Beast met when he sought shelter in his castle after being lost in the woods. When he entered, the servants were more than accommodating. He had a nice fire to warm himself by, a nice dinner composing of hot tea and the company of "uncommonalities" – a talking teacup named "Chip" and a number of talking household items. Maurice's curiosity kicked in overdrive, and as he wandered through the unfamiliar castle, he saw a rose – a beautiful rose - one that he knew his daughter Belle would appreciate. The Beast accused Maurice of thievery. Filled with rage and fury, he lashed out at Maurice! Not offering him a true chance to defend his curiosity, The Beast imprisoned Maurice for trespassing. Maurice was taken captive because he wanted to offer his beautiful daughter a rose…

I can go on about this beautiful love story – ultimately Belle and The Beast fell in love organically, and they married. The story ends after the wedding, leaving ambiguity about whether or not they live happily ever after or not… If you've ever married, or are married, then your story didn't end after the wedding, did it? No. You were never told that your handsome Prince who came in and swept you off your feet would:

- lie
- cheat
- have a child outside of your marriage
- give you an incurable disease
- drain your bank account
- abandon you
- hit you
- verbally abuse you
- deflect his anger on you
- work extra hours and come home late
- miss your anniversary, birthday, and special holidays
- be an alcoholic
- be a drug addict
- be addicted to pornography
- molest your daughter or your son
- burn you
- poison you
- accuse you
- berate you in front of family and friends

Oh, the list can go on for many pages – I'm sure you agree.

Before you clap too loud – slow down, sister, because no one ever told you that "YOU" would bring the aforementioned garbage into the marriage either. In fact, you may have had that one last sexual encounter before your wedding day, or you may have gotten pregnant from a married man and lied to your husband… Or, you might be the one who had the porn, drug, and/or alcohol addiction. You may have given your man an STD and blamed it on him, or you might be the sister who slept with his best friend/brother to get back at him… Girlfriend – come on. Yes, I know I just burst your little bubble, but keep reading – it will be a blessing to you. I trust God just that much!

Remember our friend Maurice, who was imprisoned, who was held in bondage by The Beast because he chased a rose? Remember the Beast, who was cursed, whoexperienced a form of bondage because he didn't know how to love? Let's reel this puppy in… Sister, remember when the enemy "imprisoned" you by throwing you back into the cage? The cage of anger? Bitterness? Rage? Vengeance? Emotional depression? Victim prison - he did me wrong. How about the prison of, "She took my man?" May I encourage you to stop for a second and reflect on who or what the vessel was which was used to reel you into your bondage. It could have been that you were mistreated as a child. It could have been poverty, lack, even a wayward child or husband. Your bondage could have been the perception of incompetence or inadequacy because you were not being promoted at work. In my situation, my bondage was the scarred tissue - the unaddressed residue from my childhood that kept me at the gate of the prison door! The gates were open; however, I chose to remain on the side of bondage. I literally turned my back towards the exit route, and I constantly went back to the cell of torture – emotionally. Whatever it is, let's pause for a moment to identify with the fact that it's an emotional demon. Heavenly Father, we release those emotional demons right now in the name of Jesus!

I can relate to the thoughts and actions of disruptive behaviors in relationships, marriages, parenting, and the like. However, as a woman who has endured hardship, I encourage you to begin opening the door of voluntary vulnerability. Daily, I kill the thoughts of negative emotions. I will not lie and say that it is easy – no ma'am, my struggles are just as real as yours. I choose to release my senses to the Holy Spirit. I humbly recruit His presence to use to my tongue – use me as a vessel for the edification of God's Kingdom.

> **John 3:16**
> "...for God so loved the world that He gave His only begotten Son, that whoever believes in Him should not perish but have everlasting life" (KJV).

May He receive all the glory, praise, and honor for the fruit that is yielded from this vessel. Hallelujah! I decree by faith: at this very moment, you are able to identify your prison. Now that you are able to see it for what it is – a trick of the devil, a distraction to redirect your attention, a thief of joy - Girl, get your mind back! Now! Father, in the name of Jesus: we are so grateful for your abounding love. We can never understand how much you love us because we are limited to an earthly comprehension. We release our faith to receive Your love, and to walk according to the love that you have for us. We joyfully offer our life to You as meat for Your Kingdom. Amen.

I am so proud of you! You've made a deliberate decision to reclaim your freedom, and now you get to sit back with your Holy-Spirit popcorn and watch how your life changes. Please do not make the mistake of giving up easily because of what you do not see with your physical eyes. As soon as you begin to recall negative images, release them to the Holy Spirit – cast them down immediately! Play your favorite gospel song or get your devotional scripture – the key is, "immediately…"

Chapter 19:

My Husband; My Maker

There are several people in my life whom I refer to

Ephesians 6:14-15

"Stand therefore, having your loins girt about with truth, and having on the breastplate of righteousness; and your feet shod with the preparation of the gospel of peace..."

as my spiritual teachers; they each have a purpose, and have been instrumental in being vessels to deliver God's Word audibly to me. I will never forget the day after Valentine's Day when I decided to work from home after a week filled with meetings, conference calls, extensive commute times, aching feet, and tired eyes. My husband and I are early risers – he begins his day between 3:30 and 4:30 a.m., and I usually follow suit shortly thereafter. Our routine is standard, the coffee begins brewing at 3 a.m. as we take time to read during the quiet morning hours before we succumb to the demands of our workdays - February 15th was no different. Until…

I received a call from an old friend whom I hadn't not spoken with in a couple of years – in fact, she and I had not talked since I remarried. When my phone rang, the area code looked familiar, but I couldn't connect the number with anyone I knew. I would normally ignore my phone when it rings. However, for some reason I chose to take the call… "Hello, this is Cathy," I answered.

The voice on the other end warmly stated, "Cathy {former last name}, Cathy {former last name} – oh wait, what's your new name?"

I knew exactly who it was – my friend Julia! She meant no harm. As she referenced my former married names, I burst into laughter, uncontrollably! I'm not sure why I was so tickled – maybe it was because the Holy Spirit and I were talking before Julia's call and He left me with a feeling of joy… Julia and I carried on with our cordial expressions.

In the background, I heard my other old friend Phyllis, who was screaming, "How many times is she going to get married?"

I heard Julia reply, "As many times as it takes to get it right..."

Quickly, I countered, "Nope, this is the last time – God has us!"

As Julia and I continued our conversation, I felt joyed to hear her voice! We talked about her daughter, who is the same age as my third granddaughter. We talked about our jobs, living in different cities, and her visit to my hometown of Jacksonville, Florida for the weekend. That's where she was during our call.

The topic shifted, and I heard Phyllis yell in the background, "Cathy, you need to write a book about getting married."

Julia then asked me, "Where did you and your husband meet?"

I responded, "We met on Match.com – he found me, pursued me, courted me, proposed to me, married me, and now we have the pleasure of building a life together..." I asked if either of the two had remarried or if they are dating.

Phyllis told me that she liked to date, but she had no interest in getting married. She was retired, and now all she did was travel. She told me that, once she gets tired of guys, she drops them and moves on.

I replied, "She has control issues... Blahhhhhh!"

Julia offered that she was dating as well but, but that she was only a weekend dater. She mentioned being in a relationship with one guy who was in the military, but he disappeared without a word after three months. She added that she is on the fence about dating anyone else in the military...

My husband and I are still learning each other – we have a long road ahead of us, but by the Grace of God, we are willing to try - much like any other couple, especially a new couple.

We received many compliments when we married, and the number one question was, "Where did you meet?" In fact, the question about how we met was presented to us when we were looking at rings. I replied to the questioning sales rep, "I had a flat tire on the interstate and he stopped to help me – the rest is history...." Of course, that wasn't true, but it was a damsel-in-distress story that I thought was cute. Another story of how we met is, "aisle seven at the grocery store" – we enjoyed the same coffee and we bumped into each other. That too was untrue as well, but I thought it was a cute story. The reality is, I was too embarrassed to tell our friends that we met on an online dating site, especially since relationships that are formed that way do not last - or so I was led to believe.

What Julia, Phyllis, and many others didn't know was that my husband and I were in (what I call) a development patch of our marriage. The weekend prior, we attended a marriage conference in Southlake, TX. Leading up to the conference, we seem to argue daily, and we were both at a cross-road in our marriage. The "D" word was pondered, discussed, and even attempted; however, I was hopeful that what we needed would be found at the XO Conference which was held at Gateway Church. I remember thinking to myself, *how we can be excited about hearing from God, traveling to another state, attending a spirit-filled conference, yet become so angry with each other during the conference that everything we are striving to overcome travels with us to TX, unresolved? What happened?*

John 4:18 "...for you have had five husbands..." I get so tickled when I read that scripture! Why? Because human beings are so judgmental! My husband and I met in November of 2015 and were married on January 27, 2017. We both found each other to be beautiful, amazing, fun, God-fearing, and worth giving marriage another try. We were new to each other – we sacrificed to see each other. We wanted to impress each other, and we didn't want either to feel like we were second to anything or anyone. I remember my husband's aunt giving us her blessing. As I thanked her, I offered the thought, "We are not perfect and we don't have all of the answers, but we know how not to repeat past mistakes." I was not aware of how those words would be tested, how much I'd want to walk away, nor was I aware of how may tears I'd shed, nor or how many prayers I'd offer up to God… I wasn't aware of how many times I would question my judge of character, my hasty feelings of trust, or my crave to be accepted for who I am… I did not think about the fact that my husband loved me unconditionally – I expected him to. Why? Because he said he did. But, did either of us really know what unconditional love was at the time we agreed that we wanted to spend the rest of our lives together? The answer is, "No…"

Phyllis's comment about writing a book re-ignited the passion in me to tell my story. I've made attempts in the past to write about my life, but I would become discouraged because of a certain event that I did not want to disclose. Julia's call was from the Holy Spirit – I honestly believe that - and Phyllis's comment became my assignment, "Cathy, tell your story." Out of obedience to God, and with the help of the Holy Spirit, it is my humble prayer that, as I share the details about my life, you will read with an open mind and allow God to heal you just as He has healed me. The events of my life are not meant to be forgotten – they are to be told! I am a living testimony of the goodness of God.

Father, in the name of Jesus, I pray that this book will touch the lives of women and men who have been bound by their past of shame for being in multiple marriages. No matter the reason for the divorce – release the captive! Release an anointing over the eyes reading. May the words of my story be a stepping stone for your child to come into the revelation of knowledge, understanding, and wisdom through your eyes. I thank you, Lord, for healing, delivering, and restorating in a way that releases anger, bitterness, resentment, shame, guilt, pride, arrogance, and a humble childlike crave for your presence in our lives. Thank you, Father, for the strength to carry out this task – I yield my brain, memory, hands, heart, mind, and fingers to you, and I ask that the Holy Spirit and ministering angels guide me. In the name of Jesus, I pray; Amen.

Several of my relationships were dissolved, unfulfilled, and terminated without proper closure because I resisted the urge to allow my true character to surface. What I mean in this vein is that I wasn't satisfied with who I was. According to societal standards, I was "categorized." Mixed. Lower-class. High-school dropout. Teenage parent. When I compared myself to the economic status of my influential circle – I felt I didn't fit in. A significant portion of my reality has been framed by a multitude of behaviors that I concluded to be unhealthy and unproductive for my continued growth as a Woman of God. Yet, such behaviors found themselves inside my home – my temple. Why? I would become so annoyed to hear the term "dysfunctional" until very recently. The truth is, we all have a sense of dysfunction. We grew up in different homes, with different family values - no family values for some. Naturally, anything that is abnormal from what we deem as common could potentially be considered "dysfunctional" by others. That's hilarious to me!

> ## Isaiah 54:4
>
> *"For your Maker is your Husband, the Lord of Hosts is His name; and your Redeemer is the Holy One of Israel; He is called the God of the whole earth" (NKJV).*
>
>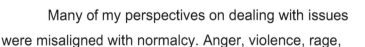

Many of my perspectives on dealing with issues were misaligned with normalcy. Anger, violence, rage, bitterness, and lacking self-control were diametrically opposed to kindness, understanding, meekness, and loving-kindness behaviors that I wanted so desperately to possess, yet knew not how… The former behaviors were a part of my life – they were second-nature responses to dealing with pain from my past (James and Kathy). When I demonstrated them, myself, they became counter-productive and non-conducive to me living a wholesome, healthy, and fulfilling life. At one point in my life, they were a non-factor - simply because I had no one to be accountable to or for other than my two daughters: Darreial and Jazz.

Domestic abuse is very damaging in many ways – even when we leave the relationship, the images are still there unless we get the right help. Women remain in battered and abusive relationships for many reasons, but there's never a "good reason." I can never understand it - although I lived it. Go figure… Throughout my forty-five-plus year of living, by the Amazing Grace of God, I have either overcome or suppressed adversities that have impacted my viewpoints and modified my definition of a normal life. I have engaged in unhealthy relationships that have challenged my emotional being as a result of my inability to identify quality core values. What are healthy relationships like? I had no clue – no example to reference when necessary… As a child, I was physically abused by both of my parents. Discipline was in the form of a plunger, a hanger, a broom, a belt, or an open (and in some cases closed) hand. Of course, the verbal abuse from my parents was just as damaging – colorful commentary such as bitch and whore were common terms from my mother as she expressed her anger towards my two sisters and me. As a teenage mother, I was physically abused by my children's father Many bruises, busted lips, and black eyes were a part of my everyday life with him, yet I was forced to sustain a relationship with a man who was four years my senior. For the first time in my life, I am disclosing the fact that I fought off a rapist, I was sexually fondled while asleep by a family friend, and I was molested by my dad. These acts are embarrassing, and I have never talked about them - why now? The reality is, everything that happened in my past that was designed to hurt me was not my fault! However, I chose to suppress memories and not address the pain, which led to subsequent pain until I opened up for healing.

My estranged relationship with my parents has been a blessing in disguise. Although I have often asked God why He chose them to be my parents, I am confident that "His Grace is sufficient," regardless of their lack of affection and abusive behaviors as parents. HIS GRACE IS SUFFICIENT! My parents were my first heartbreaks – they exposed me to behaviors that I found myself emulating. Through prayer, support, and recognition of such behaviors, I believe that I am healed, and that I have to kill thoughts of those behaviors daily. I confess – it is very challenging, especially as I age and my body changes from one phase in womanhood to another. I am confident that by the aid of the Holy Spirit, the best of Cathy is present!

Why now – why air the dirty laundry of your past, Cathy? That's an excellent question! It takes every ounce of my will-power to focus on my goal of raising awareness about abuse and suppressing negative behaviors – I am compelled to share my life story with the hope of helping at least one person. Who am I? On the profession of my faith, I am a woman who is saved by the Grace of God! I am a woman who has endured heartaches, setbacks, and rejection. I have suffered through many emotional battles, yet – I WIN! That's correct: I WIN - each time…

Black Butterfly; White Rose… One of the greatest challenges with documenting my life is disclosing my self-neglect, my painful past, and the ineffective ways that I have dealt with my internal pain. These have negatively impacted my overall way of thinking, how I interact with people. They've also affected how I reared and disciplined my children, and how I engaged in a social life. I feel physical pain – chest pain and heart palpitations - as I resurrect memories from my past, but if getting this out heals at least one person (while killing me inside): PRAISE GOD – WE WIN!

My motive for writing this book is truly genuine – it is a process for healing. I am not blind to the fact that other people have experienced common scenarios that have transpired in my life. My intent is not to devalue the relationships mentioned in this book. Rather, my intent is to raise awareness of behaviors that I observed and awareness of how the experiences have surfaced and negatively framed my adult-hood. Most importantly, my intent is to raise awareness of how not dealing with my pain by seeking proper treatment and talking through a healing process has been more harmful than anything.

I desire to inspire others by sharing intimate details of my life - some good, some not so much. I am confident that I will be successful in this effort, as men and women alike who have experienced abandonment, insecurity, low self-esteem, depression, anxiety, internal rage, and violence will identify with the fact that help is necessary for overcoming the battle - they will be inspired to seek treatment for healing immediately. It is important that I disclose a combination of events that occurred during my childhood and adulthood – if I neglect doing so, I understand that I run the risk of harboring painful memories, which, in turn, affects my ability to sustain healthy emotions. Consider this one of multiple steps necessary for proper healing.

Chapter 20:

Husband #1 - Joseph Clavizzao

I was married for the first time at, or around, twenty-four or twenty-five. This wasshortly after my kids' father and I severed ties completely. God blessed Darreial, Jazz and me with our first home when I turned 24, and I felt pretty good about dating. I met my first husband at the movies, his name was Joseph Clavizzao. He was just a charming guy, - beautiful guy. We did not date for a long time. I think we were about six months in when he asked me to marry him. I didn't know much about him; however, I was very excited that someone would even want to consider me marriage material. I later concluded that I was more excited about the word, "marriage." I didn't understand the responsibility or the purpose of marriage being something which required longevity. I knew absolutely nothing about being married - it was my first marriage. Joseph moved into my house shortly after we were married in the state of Georgia.

The marriage did not last long – maybe three or four months. I never met his mother – only his brothers Victor and his eldest brother, who was paralyzed. I received the worse news that any mother could ever hear: Darreial told me that Joseph Clavizzao molested her. When I confronted him about it, he wasted no time moving out! The second blow was that I found out that he was married to me and somebody named Annette at the same time. I was later told that Annette lived in Palm Coast Florida at that time…. Joe Clavizzao drained my bank account. He literally left me with five dollars to my name; he took all my furniture out of my house and just left. When I consulted with an attorney, he advised me to go through the legal divorce process (although it was considered polygamy).

I later went for an OB/GYN appointment, and I found out that Annette and I had the same OB/GYN – Dr. Khosravi. When I checked in for my appointment, the receptionist at the front desk recited my new last name "Clavizzao" and asked – are you married to Joe?

I replied, "Yes," with a perplexed look on my face, like, I was thinking, *how do you know my husband?*

She replied, "Congratulations, I think." She knew that Joe and Annette just had a baby boy together, and that they were still married. It was crazy!

So, technically - legally - I was not married.

But, that was a part of my life.

I don't discount it…

I have the divorce papers, which is a fluke…

Chapter 21:

Husband #2 - JC

For privacy purpose, I will not disclose my second husband's full name - I will simply refer to him as Joe. During my undergrad years in college, I met a guy who I thought was different... He pursued me and carried himself differently. He was in the Navy when we met, and he retired not too long after we graduated from college together. He was smart, articulated, structured, very attractive, and he had two kids who lived in Atlanta. I met his family. His parents were married until his mother passed away. His grandparents were married for decades, so I concluded that he had a better concept of marriage. He was family-oriented, and he seemed to have wanted to be a good husband. However, he struggled with anger management issues. We built a home together on the Westside of Jacksonville. We attended First Baptist Church of Mandarin every Sunday and every Wednesday. We were married in that church in 2001, and we taught Sunday school to married couples.

The perspectives of others were that we were a successful, progressive couple and that we lived a good life. However, behind closed doors, Joe was verbally and physically abusive. He would literally put my babies out of the house. He was very controlling; argumentative and it was draining. He was 12 years older than me and very jealous, very envious. Joe would do harmful things to me and my babies – he would change the locks on the doors of the house so that my daughters and I couldn't get in. On one occasion, he turned the water off outside while I was washing my hair because I was in the shower for too long. On another occasion, I remember that rice boiling over in the drip pan on the stove, so he took the drip pan and the eyes out of the stove to prevent me from cooking.I In another case, he put the microwave in the pantry because it was not cleaned to his standards. He provoked my anger – the anger and rage that I learned from my parents. I wasn't prepared for that kind of marriage I really needed to be in a marriage that promoted healing, the kind of marriage that promoted encouragement and spiritual prosperity, and enrichment - but I didn't know that. Joe and I lived a life of hypocrisy - I felt convicted, and made the decision to not put my children through that kind of abuse any longer. We sought counseling, and on the tail end of counseling he wrote a note. He left it on the front door, telling me that he was done, and that he didn't want to be in a marriage anymore. I took the note to our Pastor. When he read the note, he looked me square in my eyes and said, "Baby, there is nothing you can do with it. You got to let it go."

At the time, I pleaded with him, "Pastor, this is my marriage. How do I let it go? What do I do?" When I reflect, I conclude that I was afraid of the change, but that it was for the best. Joe and I eventually divorced. He later apologized, which took a lot of courage and maturity. I forgive him… He is now remarried and doing well, as far as I know.

Chapter 22:

Husband #3 - LB

My third husband LB and I were married in 2010. He taught me a lot about effective communication. Through counseling and practice with him, I learned how to take a step back and really assess the root cause of a marital dispute. During my marriage to LB, I began to see a different, better side of the woman that I was evolving into. Although we had a good friendship, I married him for all the wrong reasons. I married him because I wanted the life of being married, and I knew that he could give it to me. But I wasn't attracted to him, so I really did myself a disservice. I negatively impacted his life, his son's life, and mine… We also had differing desires when it came to a family - he wanted to have more children, but I did not. After counseling and truly assessing the health of our marriage, he finally caved. He said, "You know Cathy, I really do want to have more kids." In fairness to each-other, we gracefully severed our marriage. We walked into the courtroom holding hands, and we walked out with a hug, praying for God to forgive us as we each transitioned back into the state of being single again.

Chapter 23:

Husband #4 - My Handsome Angel, Montez

I met my current husband Montez in 2015, and we married in January of 2017. I love him dearly, and I am honored that he chose me to be his wife. My sweetheart is exactly what I asked God for (in the physical) - 5'11, 225lbs, milk chocolate caramel-coated complexion, pretty teeth, and physically fit! BAM! Talk about restoration... Won't he do it!?!? However, Montez and I are like two rough stones rubbing against each other to smooth out our surfaces – I giggle as I type, but it's true!

I declared to myself that I will never lie again about the challenges of being married. It is beautiful to share your life with another person, but it is work! Montez and I have many differences - we have different communication styles, hobbies, daily routines, and professions (to name a few).Nonetheless, he is one of God's greatest blessings to me! He tries, and that means the world to me. We are still early in our marriage – a little over two years in, and we have a long way to go. We do not have all the answers, but we know what hasn't worked in our past relationships, and we work hard to avoid repeating past mistakes.

- Have we talked about giving up?
- Yes!
- Do we argue?
- Yes!
- Are we perfect?
- NOT by a long shot!
- Do we get discouraged?
- YES!

Why do I want you to know these things? Because, once again, we have to die to our fleshly tendencies, daily! I am not ashamed to share that this is my 4th marriage, and I am committed to being the best wife (IN CHIRST) that I can be. I am committed to doing my best to nurture the gift that God has given me that lies inside of my husband, and when I meet my Father face-to-face, I will be able to give an account for how I cared for the gift in him..

This time around, I've chosen to release my marriage and my husband to God. I will not unfairly ask Montez to be what I needed from James and Kathy. He is own man, and as long as I yield to the instruction of the Holy Spirit and do my part to be the best wife according to scripture, I am truly in the safe zone. My marriage therapy comes from many sources:

 Titus 2:3-5

"...The aged women likewise, that they be in behavior as becometh holiness, not false accusers, not given too much wine, teachers of good things; that they may teach the young women to be sober, to love their husbands, to love their children, to be discreet, chaste, keepers at home, good, obedient to their husbands, that the word of God not be blasphemed" (KJV).

- ❧ Prayer – releasing the negativity
- ❧ Talking openly with other believers
- ❧ Tapping into people who've experienced similar situations
- ❧ Surrounding myself with a strong source of accountability partners

I love Jim and Karen Evans as well as David and Ashley Willis - they've been there! They talk about having a naked marriage - being vulnerable and opening the door for health and healing, having a healthy sex life, and learning how to bridge gaps in communication as a married couple. When two people come from extremely dysfunctional backgrounds - when they have learned to expect abandonment from those closest to them - their defense mechanisms become the norm. We can never heal that way, much less have progress. In my current marriage, I've recruited wisdom, revelation knowledge, understanding, and the mind and character of Christ. I am in His will when Montez and I are working through an issue.

I have my husband's best interests at heart, and I love the fact that God has trusted me with him. When I am discouraged because of what my physical eyes see, a simple prayer and comfort from the Holy Spirit offers me something totally different shining down from the spiritual realm. Oh, what great glory the kingdom will receive should I continue to lift my husband up to him! One thing is for sure – he has a praying wife and a strong accountability partner, and I trust in God daily that He will bless my marriage.

Montez Franklin – you are my #1; I am grateful for your partnership on this journey! I am grateful that you are Sexy, too – how about that?!?! A little humor here (smile).

Chapter 24:

A Message of Hope for Marriage

If you are praying for a husband, then make it a daily part of your prayer life to pray for your strength in the Lord – for both of you! Also, seek counseling, because we all have a dark past that we must let go of in order to be the best spouse that God has called us to be. Enter marriage with an open mind, understand that you will have differences. Offer GRACE, patience, and when you are weak in faith – be quiet. Pray. Drop the guards, and let God do what He does best, which is HIS BEST! Most importantly, if you are in an abusive or adulterous marriage – GET HELP, immediately. I believe that everything is forgivable, but pray for God to guide you…

Chapter 25:

Grace in the Crossfire

Oh, what a blessing it is to know that my God never gives up on me. I have the choice to yield to the promptings of the Holy Spirit, to trust in the promises of God – to serve Him. I choose not run when I am in the crossfire of attacks, whether they are involve my marriage, my health, my children, my finances, my job, or battles of insecurities which flood my mind! We have a choice to answer, "Yes," to questions

> **Isaiah 45:3**
>
> *"I will give you the treasures of darkness and hidden recheck of secret places that you may know that I, the LORD, Who call you by your name am the God of Israel"*
>
> *(NKJV).*

that the enemy uses against us – you know -, the ones that convenient attack us while we're in the shower, the ones that cause us to see those crowfoot extensions as we apply that mascara, even the ones that randomly pop up during the commute to the office – yea, those...

They sound like... *Am I good enough? Did I do a job good enough to meet the "expectations" of others? Am I the right size? Am I pretty enough? Am I articulate enough? Educated enough? Experienced, credentialed or skilled enough? Is my skin light or dark enough?* The list goes on, but when does it end?

Beloved, lean in and read closely - find solace in 1 Corinthians 15:10, "But whatever I am now, it is all because God poured out his special favor on me – and not without results. For I have worked harder than any of the other apostles; yet it was not I but GOD who was working through me by His Grace" (NLT). My dear sister, if scripture tells us that it is by God's grace that we are who we are, then we can confidently affirm our positions as daughters of the Most High King. I must admit, I found it hard in the beginning because I wasn't as strong in my faith. Although I am still growing, I am strong enough, now, to know that I cannot allow the enemy to use my self-doubts against me. NO! Today - in fact - at this very moment – I encourage you to yield your senses to the Holy Spirit so that they may be used as meat for the Kingdom of God. Let every thought, word, expression, and deed be delivered with caution, because lives are at stake. The enemy is observing our Character, and as soon as we demonstrate a lack of self-control, the enemy adds condemnation to our shopping carts, a condemnation that can never be checked out unless we yield our senses.

Just as I began working on this project, I found myself within two feet of the crossfire. My husband planned a trip to Baltimore, and it seemed like we were engaging in verbal conflict daily – for weeks! Oh my goodness, you know those arguments that surface when you take the ring off and pray to God that he never returns again? I slept in the middle of the bed, turned the air down to 65 degrees, rolled out of bed when I wanted too, enjoyed my coffee alone, and then it hit me – CROSSFIRE! Don't judge me, I repented for the negative thinking and speaking. I am a work in progress – praise God. It was during that time that the Holy Spirit introduced the scripture Isaiah 45:3 "…there are treasures in dark places and hidden riches of secret places." I can honestly share that darkness with which I have become closely acquainted, and I have a choice to remain there or to let the light of my Lord and Savior shine so bright that I reclaim my purpose and joy in HIM. My

John 8:12

"When Jesus spoke again to the people, He said, 'I am the light of the world. Whoever follows me will never walk in darkness, but will have the light of life.'" (NIV).

choice is NOT to dwell in those dark places… My choice is to diligently seek the light of the world, Jesus Christ.

Chapter 26:

Breaking the Generational Curse

I am intentional with sharing details about my life – through my lens - with the hope that others draw the following conclusions: (a) it's ok to be vulnerable, (b) you are not alone, and (c) I chose to heal and now I must help others – it's my assignment! I am very passionate about younger women – especially my daughters, who are now mothers. In fact, I sent them a text not too long ago, telling them that I wish I had a mother like them – they are simply crushing this motherhood thing and doing it very well! Not only do I love my daughters, I respect them, and I want to see them continue to do well. They are a gift, and I am held accountable for how I nurture, coach, and guide my daughters – from cradle to grave.

What's different about me?

What did I learn from Kathy?

I am grateful for the opportunity to be a mother. I wasn't aware of the task at hand because I was a child when I became a mom - I did not know the severity of the responsibility of raising another human being, much less of raising another daughter. Doing so has reassured me that God's presence is real, and and that he has such an amazing plan for our lives. So, no matter what I thought I would do as a young mother, His plan was to trump my plan like nobody's business. I knew what it was like to "not know" who my mother was – I am deliberate in sharing details about my life with my daughters (and my husband). Sometimes, I'll have a random thought about my past, and I'll strike up a conversation with either of the three to get the issue out in the open. My two greatest challenges are motherhood and being a wife – I am still learning both, to be honest. Because my daughters are adults now, my responsibility has shifted from acting as an authoritative figure to being a coach, a mentor, and a guide – an accountability partner, if you will…

I take full responsibility for being different – being better! I know who I am in Christ, and that helps… Every now and then, I have to rebuke the spirit of lack. At times, I've questioned myself. *Am I enough? Am I smart enough?* The answer to both of these is, "Yes – I am! I choose, daily, to fight against the images of insecurity – against the thoughts of lining up with the expectations of others. Self-insecurity and doubt are an awful place of darkness - being concerned with the thoughts of how someone else views me is equally as bad! When I wake up in the morning, I am purposeful in yielding my knowledge gates to the sound, the voice, the instruction, and the guidance of Christ and the Holy Spirit. If that is truly my focus, why do I care about what other people think? I have to check myself whenever those negative thoughts come about. That's what's different about me today, compared to the me of my past. I now view the phases of my life differently, and I no longer blame James and Kathy McDade (nor do I blame my former husbands).

Chapter 27:

My Unique Identity

I did not receive a Harvard education - because of my circumstances as a teenage mother, as a child, I made the decision to stop going to school to care for my daughter. I eventually went to night school while working at a fast-food restaurant, and earned my GED. I also earned an AA from Florida Community College at Jacksonville, a BBA from Edward Waters College, and an MA from Webster University. There were times when I took my daughters to night school with me – I ran the risk of being sent home, but my instructors were compassionate enough to let us learn together.

Sometimes I ask myself, did I go to the best schools? Did I receive the best credentials? Then I have to check myself and say, it was by the grace of God that somebody was in that path to say you're a good candidate for this. And then again, I have to do another double-check to say, why do I need to meet the expectations of others? Who created the standard of intellect, or wit, or ability, or competence? Who said that I have to fit this category to be confident or competent or exceptional or extraordinary in

that area? Who did that? Christ accepts me for who I am –
I am His image! And, that's good enough for me!

I was made to stand out, not to fit in!

I am not made to succumb to what society says or
thinks about my intellect, my level of experience, or what I
bring to the table. What I bring to the table is a genuine
perspective of where I've been, and I am able to coach
people who are willing to dive deep into their past for
healing – I can only do that with the help of the Holy Spirit
along with their willingness to let go of the past. Above all, I
would tap into Scripture – whatever we face, my motto is,
"there's a scripture for that!"

Chapter 28:

Parents, Let's Help our Children

I believe that, as parents, it is our responsibility to help our children identify with who they are. Begin with complimenting:

- ♣ You are the child of the Most High King!
- ♣ You are my baby!
- ♣ You are my blessing - my angel!
- ♣ I am grateful to God for trusting me with you!
- ♣ You are my gift!
- ♣ I am here for you…
- ♣ We are in this together…

As parents, we plant seeds of hope (or doubt), and society will greet our babies with a different perspective of their identify – trust me! Check out social media today – what a trap… Especially for our daughters…

In the spirit of transparency, in many cases, I missed the mark, when my daughters were smaller. I thought I was very strategic and doing the right things - I would always do their hair. They always had earrings. They were jewels. They had nice clothing. They had clean underwear that didn't have holes. They looked like little girls, however, when it came to their identity – I missed the opportunity to nurture them. I have since learned the importance of affirmation and of encouraging the formation of my daughters' identity. Affirming our children is so important. Ss mothers, if we miss this part of child-rearing years, we leave the door open for other entities to come in – and I'm speaking from experience (remember my kids' father, Darrell? That's how he was able to get to me). If you missed the mark on affirming your child in the past, I urge you to begin today by correcting it, or else the enemy will come in and plant seeds of doubt. It will become harder for your prince or princess to find themselves when they are older, so affirm that you will do your best as a parent to make sure that your babies have everything they need, within reason - bridge those gaps between uncertainty and certainty.

What I mean by bridging gaps between uncertainty and certainty is, from a little girl's perspective (through Cathy's lens):

* I'm uncertain about what the world looks at me as or who the world looks at me as.

❧ I know for certain what my mom looks at me as, and who she looks at me as.

As mothers, we takee responsibility to make sure that, every single day - or as often as we think about it - we are encouraging our daughters. We are standing up for our daughters. When we encourage and affirm them at home, they are prepared for the flying darts in the real world.

It's a blessing when your daughter is vulnerable towards you as a parent! There is no greater joy than for a little girl to be able to come to her mom - very vulnerable and very open - and say, "You know what mom, they hurt me," "I don't look like them," or, "They don't accept me, but you do – thank you mom (or dad)." What a beautiful feeling it is to be able to give your baby a hug of comfort. Nurture and protect – that's our job as parents. When we truly understand the nurturing and protection component of parenting, I believe that our children will be able to identify with who they are, and in the proper priority. Once they develop that positive self-identification, decision making about acceptance based on their levels of security in their identity becomes second-nature. On the opposing side – remember the chaos from my childhood? As a result of negative self-identification, I began to live like my parents – acceptance for abusive behavior became normal because that's what I knew.

...So, parents, think about the reverse. The healthy nurturing, the loving-kindness, and the gentle loving touches that only a parent can deliver are worth more to your child – especially during the development and influential years. We are human beings who respond to touch. Mothers, as we touch our daughters, we are transferring energy. When we touch them in a loving manner – the anointing flows when the energy is positive.

Mothers, it is our responsibility to help our daughters develop a firm knowledge of their identity – they are more than the opinions of social media images and standards. Encourage your children to accept who they are in Christ - whether they are light, dark, black, brown, pale, white, rustic, or red. I become very passionate about casting down what society views as beauty defined by social media, and what others say a woman should look like. Satan is very strategic, and he will sneak in very subtly, encouraging us to augment who we are naturally until we are unable to accept our original selves as beautiful... Think about it for a second... Was it the woman or man who influenced the bigger:

- Breast
- Butt, or
- smaller waistline?
- Where did that start?

May I encourage you to share with your children (and consider the thought for yourself) that God designed every cell of your body, and he designed every hair on your head - grey hair and split ends, too. He created your legs to be shaped a certain way just like your waste, your breasts, your shoulders, and your posture. He created it! Never give anyone the authority to determine what mold you fit in… Trust that you fit in God's mold…

As parents, we are responsible for our children, and we owe them a nurturing, protective environment – free from any form of abuse! If this was/is your pattern – it is not too late to make a change. Begin with a prayer and heartfelt cry out to God, and welcome His healing power. Next, apologize to your child for being abusive – open the door for the conversation. Allow them to be angry – they have to get their feelings out, too! A good next step is to seek counseling.

Chapter 29:

Message to Fathers

From a daughter (the little girl in me) to a father (the daddy in you), please love, nurture, and protect your children. If you have a little girl, especially, set the stage for her so that she doesn't default to a thug! Your babies need you! We have an outline of what the family structure is supposed to be about - it is in the word. God instructs fathers not to provoke their children's wrath, lest they be discouraged. What typically happens when we become discouraged as adults? We default to anger, sadness, or addictive behaviors – think about what happens to a child under those circumstances…

- I never showed my child how to smoke weed
- I never showed my child how to snort a line
- I never showed my child how to be a prostitute
- I never showed my child how to be an alcoholic
- I never showed my child how to do all the things that don't align with what happened in the home.
- What <u>you did</u> show your child is that they could not come to you.

* If they could not depend on you to provide a platform for them to be vulnerable towards you, then they defaulted to what was accepted of them, and to who accepted them.

If you are a father and you have a daughter, then show her how special she is. Buy her the cutest little dress. Take her on her first date. Show here what values to look for in a man, please... Next, kick it up a notch by demonstrating loving-kindness towards her mother or your wife in the home. Make it a common practice to date your daughter - have ice cream with her; talk with her. Share things with her from a man's perspective in two different variables. And, for the love of God – put the phone down when you are with her!

When your daughter begins to take interest in boys she will need a baseline – you are it, Mr. She will start to look at men and, to a degree, make a comparison, "If my dad did this and it made me feel good, then this is what I'm looking for my potential mate." Additional work will be required because, when she marries, you don't want her looking at her husband as a father - There will be some required coaching. Again, if this works on the positive side of the spectrum, think about how it works on the negative side of the spectrum. If you are physically abusive, verbally abusive, or if you default to substance abuse instead of solving problems through prayer and counseling, what do you think your daughter's default will be? I can tell you, brother, she will default to that same behavior. In my opinion, men really don't understand the level of influence that they have on the life of a little girl, nor do they understand how delicate the time spent with that girl is. I never had a boy, so I can't speak to that level of experience. What I can say, however, is based on the fact that I'm married, and I see some of the development opportunity with some of the men that I interact with.

Husbands, let's talk about being more sensitive and empathetic towards your wife or future wife – for the sake of the children. Women are estrogen-driven - we desire to nurture affection and emotional connectivity. We appreciate your strength, and we need that in you! It's also important to note that you cannot be everything to us (as men), and we have to find that proper balance. When we do come to you for love and attention, it usually begins with a friendly conversation – please resist the urge to go into fix-it mode, because what is needed at that time is a demonstration of love…

* Husbands, that tidbit of information will enhance your life of intimacy

Chapter 30:

Identity and Cosmetic Enhancements

Why do we allow the opinions of others to encourage thoughts of augmenting our bodies? Why do we succumb to the crave to be physically accepted by meet the expectations of others? Consider the fact that the person influencing you to augment your body may not be in your life after the augmentation takes place. So, why go through the pain - the torture - of changing who you are to accommodate someone who may not be here tomorrow?

Let's just nip this in the bud and says, at least for Cathy (myself), I have been the victim of the cosmetic procedures. I had breast implants at 32, and I wish I'd never done it - I really do. I lost the volume of my breasts, and they were flat - I felt insecure. I wanted them lifted - perkier. No one ever warned me about the psychological effects behind doing something like that. No one ever said that your body is to respond emotionally to a foreign object in it.

Externally, what we see are nice breasts.

Internally, I'm in pain because my body is different.

I share this part of my life because of what our younger generation sees as beauty. What's happening when our girls, our women of today, are captivated with the images on social media and they succumb to body argumentation? They do not anticipate the emotional hound - the regret. We rarely hear people talk about that. One of my friends told me about a guy who shared with her how he seems attracted to women who enhance their bodies, but not romantically. He further went on to say that most men are drawn to the fantasy in their minds, but when it comes to what they want at home – it's a different look. May I pause here for a moment and encourage women not to enhance their bodies for a man – please… Love yourself enough…

It's a weird dynamic because my husband said it doesn't feel the same. It feels fake. Women think, if you are drawn to this - attracted to this - then why wouldn't I get it? So you open up with your story with so much needed dialogue on self-love, identity, why we do what we do, and about being able to share your story. Cathy, to be honest with you - Yes, I do see your platform around.

There are certain exceptions for everything – like a breast cancer patient who desires to reconstruct her breast to maintain femininity - that's different... What I am referring to right now is the vanity stages of life... I would say we are taught - we're definitely, definitely taught - what's important about identity. There are variations of identity, but this is just Cathy's opinion.

There are variations of identity. We have the physical identity, and we have the intellectual, emotional, and mental identity. What's more important? We really have to get to a place in life where we start educating at a greater level. The world of entertainment is a cycle, in my opinion, on their moral values, debauchery, and slander - it is a repetitive cycle of vanity at the expense of rejection and of trying to fit in based on a standard established by "a mere man."

These social media images of celebrity lifestyles and looks are setting the upcoming generations up for false expectations. Think about it from this perspective - you can constantly augment your physical appearance to the point that your augmentations are no longer attractive. For the mild case of enhancement – it may not be that bad; however, for the extremist who is never satisfied - look at before and after pictures...

Now what?

Love who you are, please....

We have to get better and reclaim our identity!

You are a beautiful person!

Period!

I admit - sometimes, I question myself. I'm like, *oh my God, I am aging.* Then, I have to take a step back. It depends on the day. Am I wearing my little braids and feeling youthfully cute, or did I wake up and see fluid build-up in my face? It's a battle that I have to cast down, daily! I will tell myself, *drink some water girlfriend!* Ha, ha! I have really accepted that this is what I look like. This is who I am; this is how I talk. These are my facial expressions. I mean, this is just who I am. I have encouraged my daughters to do the same thing as well. Accept who you are – you beautiful angel.

Chapter 31:

Overcoming Identity Crisis

I am fourty-six years young, and I am able to look at the way my body has changed - the way my facial features have changed. My freckles are a little bit morepronounced (Giggle). Yes, my freckles are a little bit more pronounced than they were when I was a kid. I still battle with my hair. Ugh, my hair and I have a love-hate relationship! I've gone short, I've gone long. Right now, my hair is in two braids. I feel like, *OK, this is me.* Now, I even have braces as an adult. I began menopause at thirty-eight years young, and I still learn things about my body that I never knew about before! I was clueless – no one prepared me!

- I love the woman that I have become!
- I love the woman that God loves!
- I love me!
- … it took a long time to say that… Cathy, I love you, girl! You fricken rock!
- Your high cheekbones

✤ Your little pug nose – girl, you rock it!

When I was a kid, I hated my nose! I remember being teased about my nose in school because I have a split in the middle of my nose – one kid told me that my nose looked like a butt. How silly! As I type and look in the mirror, I become fonder of my nose – God gave it to me!

> # 1 Corinthians 15:10
>
> *"But by the grace of God, I am what I am; and His grace which was bestowed upon me was not in vain..."*
>
> *(KJV)*
>
>

Chapter 32:

To Those Who Struggle with Identity

It is by the grace of God that you are who you are. I've concluded that, when people try to categorize you, it could mean one of two things: (a) they really admire you or (b) they are deflecting their insecurities upon you. May I encourage you to always choose what God says about you! Beginning today, make it a practice to love on you! It is unfair for you to expect anyone else to love you if you are not open to receiving the love of Christ, first. The next step is disciplining yourself to "love yourself" enough by accepting the beautiful person that you are, and to stop comparing yourself with others.

Part 3:

It's Time to Transform!

Chapter 33:

Crawling Out of the Caccoon

I've shared a lot of darkness from my life. I've also shared the importance of recognizing it and getting the proper help. Now let's talk about letting it go – for good! If you do not, your past will.

Let's begin:

- Healing is refreshing!
- Give yourself permission to let go!
- Be grateful for your past.
- Know that the pain is real – the trauma is real.
- Do not act as if nothing happened.
- Use your time wisely to process the actions/trauma that have affected you.
- Talk freely and openly – it will be a form of healing and reflection.

You are exactly where God wants you to be in this very moment – it may not seem like it, but it's true... You're reading this book! He has a way of bringing us through these experiences for teachable moments – you are now in student mode… However, your experience will position you to operate in teacher mode. Remember that, earlier, I shared a scripture that tells us of the same comfort that God comforts us with – we are to comfort others.

Remember that, earlier, we talked about the process of the caterpillar transforming into a butterfly? Well - you, too, are now in your transformative phase. Inside the cocoon, the caterpillar liquefies its tissue – that's painful! The body is being broken down so that it can repair itself for its intended purpose – to feed the earth!

- Go on, cover girl – you are preparing to feed the earth!
- It's beautiful!
- Yea, you!
- Your wings are forming right now…
    - Go on and cry if you have too
    - Write down your feelings
    - Seek counseling
    - Pray for a prayer partner
    - And, let's move forward – boldly!

Butterflies are drawn to flowers, and butterflies have a significant role in pollinating. You are delicate and fragile just like flowers that rely on their environment. You are changed a lot, and the butterfly represents this metamorphosis and beauty demanding your attention. My dear, you will now begin to attract other butterflies. Together, you will feed the earth – one daughter at a time - so preparation and healing stages are critical.

The pressure of being in a cocoon, I'd imagine, is painful - the body of the caterpillar swells, liquifies, reproduces its cells, and ultimately outgrows its cocoon environment.

* Transformation takes place in painful moments

Chapter 34:

The Wheel of Transformation

    Going through a healing process forces us to stand out. As you heal, you will sense rejection because you are navigating the waters of finding your new fit. Remember when you rested securely in the familiarity of your past dysfunction? Whether it was the abuse, identity crisis, teen parenthood, multiple marriages – whatever the case, it was familiar to you and you were comfortable there... Now, it's time to change things in your life for the better, and my dear, it will be different. Confusing at times... Painful at times... Scary at times... But guess what? That means you are growing!

    We all have a responsibility towards each other. You are my sister (and brother) in Christ. I am honored to have been the vessel used to address pain, suffering, and hardship – all while the Glory of the Lord rested on my life. Now, I share with you my "transformation" process...

You don't fit in, you stand out! Release your emotions right now, and grab a hold of what the word of God says that you are. Allow the Holy Spirit to guide you into who you should be. When I battled with my identity crisis, one of my struggles was fitting it – but why? I will never fit into a society that does not honor God. Fom a worldly perspective, when we struggle to find ourselves, we default to what the world standards are for our lives – this is where the enemy grabs a hold of our thinking and he has a field day with it!

Romans 12:2

"And be not conformed to this world; but be ye transformed by the renewing of your mind, that ye may prove what is that good, acceptable, and perfect will of God"

(KJV).

Where do we being? With a heart of purpose! Stand out with purpose – for the sake of the next generation of women.

Typically, when you're in a birthing season - yes, there are lots of changes. You're shedding the of skin of the past and coming into a new life! Transformation is intentional, beautiful, and purposeful… Everything that happened in my past was designed by God as a platform for me to serve others – what an honor! It's really a gift to help someone heal through my life stories.

We do not transform by discounting our pain as if it did not take place, or as if certain events didn't occur in our lives. Rather, we transform by pressing our way through the birthing canal. When we get to the other side of the trauma, the air is different... I think about how a baby breathes while in the mother's womb – it breathes fluid, right? Even a baby endures pain as it travels through the birthing walls, and when the birthing process has been completed, the baby breaths in a new manner – through air!

Think of a flower that survived and grew through a crack in the concrete – the odds of survival were against that flower, right? When we are determined to grow, natural elements will find their way in to nurture us – that's how God works...

When my friend offered to help me with this project, I was overwhelmed – I didn't know where to begin or how to pull the pieces of this puzzle together. I remember telling her that we are partners, that we are the joint vessels to deliver a message of healing and hope, "God's divine moment has presented itself."

So, let's transition into the "**Wheel of Transformation**."

- Spiritual Responsibility (Authority)
- Accountability Responsibility

- Health & Wellness
- Financial Stewardship

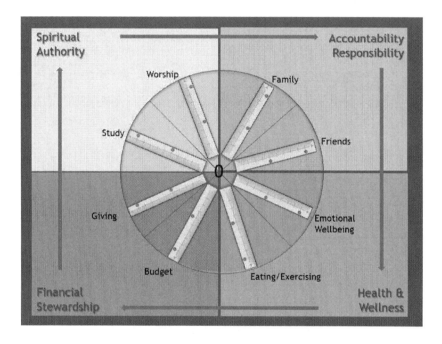

As a Certified Life Coach, I became familiar with the "Wheel of Life." As I prayed about the best way to use it, I was led to enhance it using four key pillars. Feel free to chart where you are on a scale from 0 – 10 (zero is at the center of the circle, and ten is at its cicrumference). Each spec on the ruler-looking-lines represents a number. The first red dot is "5," and the second red dot (closer to the circumference) is a "10." For each area, plot your level of participation. For example, on a scale of 0-10, I would plot myself at a 5 for eating and exercising in the "Health & Wellness" category. For me, that is an area that I'd like to improve in. However, I'd plot myself at an 8 in the "Spiritual Authority" category, because I do not allow anything to disrupt my flow of studying. Once you've plotted your circle, connect the dots. You will be able to determine where you are focused more and where you can improve. Next, determine how you'd like to improve in the areas that you are less strong. For me, it would be maintaining a purpose in exercising. Don't work out for a week and then stop, keep going for optimal results.

❧ Cathy's Current Wheel: I need a better balance in the area of exercising and eating.

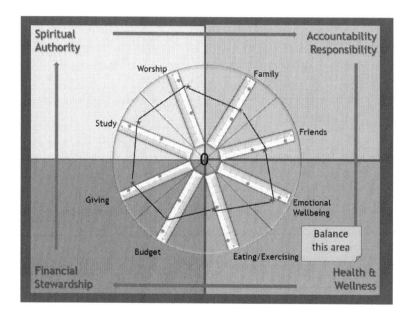

Chapter 35:

Spiritual Responsibility (Authority)

In your own time, camp out in Luke 13:10-17. There, you will find the story of a woman who had been crippled by a spirit for eighteen years. When Jesus saw her, he called her forward and said to her, "Woman, you are set free from your infirmity." Then, he put his hands on her - immediately, she straightened up and praised God. Sister, every issue that we face was nailed to Calvary and we have been cleansed of all unrighteousness when our Lord and Savior Jesus Christ offered his body, his blood, and his unconditional love for the redemption of our sins. Do you know what that means? It means you are free! God our Father saw into our future. He called his Son Jesus into being, where he was obedient to His calling to the cross, and HE SAID, "It is finished" (John 19:30). That means your ability to overcome the internal imprisonment of emotional turmoil has been given – now receive it. You should not be surprised when people identify you with who you used to be:

- Angry Angela
- Scorned Samantha
- Revengeful Rebecca
- Bloodthirsty Beverly
- Crazy Cathy – LOL!

May I encourage you to find comfort in knowing that in Luke 13:16 Jesus defended the woman who had been afflicted – in fact, he said to the synagogue leader who basically called Jesus out for healing on the Sabbath, "Then should not this woman, a daughter of Abraham, whom Satan has kept bound for eighteen long years, be set free on the Sabbath day from what bound her?" One of the most beautiful parts of this revelation is knowing where the bondage came from – clearly, scripture tells us. From Satan! The good news is that there are many scripture references for healing. In order to heal, however, you must know what the Word says about it. That's why it's imperative to combine quality study time with worship, and to let the Lord reveal what you need to do.

I

Worship

Scriptures:

🦋 **I Samuel 1:19** *"...and, they rose up in the morning early, and worshipped before the Lord, and returned, and came to their house to Ramah: and Elkanah knew Hannah his wife; and the Lord remembered her."*

🦋 **I Samuel 15:25** *"Now, therefore, I pray thee, pardon my sin, and turn again with me, that I may worship the Lord."*

II

Study

Scriptures:

- ♣ 2 Timothy 2:15 "'Study' to show thyself approved unto God, a workman that needed not to be ashamed, rightly diving the word of truth."
- ♣ 1 Thessalonians 4:11 "…and, that ye study to be quiet, and to do your own business, and to work with your own hands…"

Chapter 36:

Accountability Responsibility - Parnterships for Healing

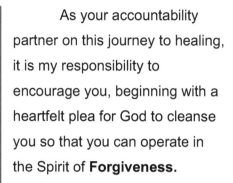

Luke 11:4

"And forgive us our sins, For we also forgive everyone who is indebted to us. And do not lead us into temptation but deliver us from the evil one" (NKJV).

As your accountability partner on this journey to healing, it is my responsibility to encourage you, beginning with a heartfelt plea for God to cleanse you so that you can operate in the Spirit of **Forgiveness.**

🦋 Yes, the BIG "F" WORD!
🦋 You are healed in the name of Jesus!

Sister, there are many details about my life that remain a mystery, and it is my prayer that God will reveal only the important factors to me for the sole purposes of edifying His Kingdom while I continue to develop in my faith journey. My childhood was an absolute mess – in the eyes of a mere man – but God!

The "ditch" which was a stream of water in our backyard that my sisters and I played in quite often. I remember, as a child during hurricane season, our backyard would look like a river when the ditch would fill to capacity – it would creep into our yard, and it took days for the water to recede. We had a large oak tree in our front yard, and being the active little girl that I was, I'd climb the tree – pretend it was my tree house; I would flip on the branches and jump from the top of the tree. It's only the by the grace of God that I never broke a bone, because I was always flipping or doing cartwheels off something... Most would say that I was "tomboyish," although I am not sure what that really meant – I was simply an inquisitive little girl who found ways to occupy my time outside which protected me from the demons inside. Like most people, if not all, I asked God – why did He give me my parents? They did not seem to be the ideal fit for me or for each other, either, for that matter. My childhood was not ideal; neither were my early adulthood years. I was a teen mom with two kids by 20, and I had multiple marriages... I can no longer blame my parents for life – I choose to forgive, and I encourage you to do the same. I now hold you accountabile for opening your heart and inviting the love of God in, so that you can walk in the blessing that He's plotted out – just for you! Release the anger, release the tension, and create the environment that you want - an environment that welcomes the presence of the Holy Spirit, not the hound of hell! Let it go!

Are you aware scripture tells us that Satan roams the earth seeking whom he can devour, and it is his desire to sift us like wheat? He has no regard for our feelings, he has no regard for our purpose in life - he wants to destroy us. The Bible talks about how God granted permission for certain things to happen – read the book of Job! The enemy says, "I am going to strip this person to the core," and he has fun doing it!

But God!

As soon as the enemy is a centimeter from the core of his victim, God steps in and says, "That's enough," before he can get to the core. For me, that would be my breaking point. God's mercy is so profound in that stage – I have felt like He's told me in those moments, "Cathy, now I've got you at your most vulnerable - now I can work through you."

I've learned that all I can do during testing time is praise my way through until God is ready to release me. Is it hard? Yes, at times, depending on the situation. It was especially hard when I was in my most broken state of being, but God wanted to use me in that space... I was broken - absolutely broken! That's exactly where He wanted me to be. When I focused on the problem instead of Him, the process of healing was delayed. I didn't see His wonder-working power until this stage in my life. Praise His Holy name! I am honored to have experienced my past – through the love of Christ, I now have a story to help someone else. It was a very small fraction of my life, but the hardships were for the sake of somebody else getting their healing, their deliverance, their restoration. Just being able to redirect that person - specifically that woman - who questions who she is in her life at 50, at 60, at 80. What is my purpose? Why am I here?

I can talk about my small, fragmented life for the hope of her healing by the grace of God. That, to me, is the joy. Oh my God, it is the joy. This was a form of therapy - just to talk through it - because sometimes I do question if it is the right moment. Do I really want to open up that shell? So many people have looked at me and would never guess I'm the mother of a 31-year-old child. "How did that come about?" I can picture them asking. I can't automatically say, "Oh, I got pregnant at 13," you know? That's not the right audience - it's not the right timing. This gives me an opportunity to really be unashamed, you know? I read about that this morning, Psalms 45. I'm grateful that I am out of that dark spot.

III

Family

Scriptures:

- **1 Corinthians 7:3** *"Let the husband render unto the wife due benevolence: and, likewise also the wife unto the husband."*

- **Colossians 3:18-21** *"Wives, submit to your own husband, as it is fitting in the Lord. Husbands, love your wives and do not be bitter toward them. Children, obey your parents in all things, for this is well-pleasing to the Lord. Fathers, do not provoke your children, lest they become discouraged."*

IV

Friends:

Scriptures:

🍂 **Job 42:10** *"And the Lord turned the captivity of Job when he prayed for his friends: also, the Lord gave Job twice as much as he had before."*

🍂 **Proverbs 18:24** *"A man that hath friends must shew himself friendly: and there is a friend that sticketh closer than a brother."*

Chapter 37:

Health & Wellness - Your Temple

V

Emotional Well-being

I am of the mindset that physical scars can be covered up - they will even heal, in time, as our bodies are naturally designed to rebuild themselves. However, internal scars will require a greater layer of faith and persistence in overcoming the issue that caused them as well as a daily confession of healing. My soul has chosen to put the hands of each person who has physically touched me in an inappropriate way on the throne of GRACE! Both the Old and New Testament are filled with supporting scriptures of God's healing power for our external ailments. He is the same God today as He was yesterday.

My childhood scars left me questioning who I am. At this point in my life, I am very grateful that I have gotten to a place where I can sense when I'm getting off balance. Every single day, I am a work in progress; I have to resist the urge to say, *oh maybe I should chisel this or I maybe I should do that.* The right thing to do is to balance the a good diet through food and exercise. I do my absolute best to eat the proper fruit and vegetables. My body is shaped the way it is because this is how God designed me. It is healthy to drink X ounces of water. I do that to help hydrate my skin. I have to take care of my Temple, and I can't allow social media, the entertainment industry, nor my past to force me to devalue you - the beautiful person that I am.

When I was a kid, I remember that set of mirrors in our old house that I told you about earlier, and how James (my dad) told me that I was ugly when I would brush my hair, looking into those mirrors with crooked teeth. Every now and again, I hear that – especially when I am dealing with my hair – go figure!

It is a trick of the devil!

An emotional scar that I have been delivered from

I am healed!

VI

Eating/Exercising

I am not suggesting that we become bodybuilders, but if that is your thing – go for it! What I am suggesting is that you put some cardio in your routine. Do what you have to do to make sure that your heart rate is healthy and your blood pressure is regulated properly. Think about healthy living for health reasons. Develop healthy habits instead of augmenting your appearance.

Chapter 38:

Financial Stewardship - Give and it Shall be Given!

I would love to invite you in on a testimony – especially as it pertains to this project. As I began preparing for the, "When Women Heal Global Leadership Summit, I looked at the costs associated with the trip, and thought – oh no, not right now... I prayed, and I asked God to reveal to me if I should attend, am I in His will – show me... My dear, if you don't want to hear from God – don't ask, because He speaks in unique ways...

I set up a GoFundMe page and talked about a highly condensed version of the material shared in this book. I set a goal for $8,500 and sent the link to a few people on LinkedIn along with a few email messages to a couple co-workers. I became very discouraged. The next day, I prayed, "Lord, who can I bless?" I sent my girlfriend a text – just saying hello.

She replied, "Hi, my sister just passed away – I need to get to Canada! I will call you later..."

I responded, "I am so sorry for your loss, how can I help?"

She admitted, "The flights are just so expensive, almost $800."

I paused and said, *God, is this your way of telling me to sow?*

God replied, *Cathy, buy the plane ticket,* and I didn't hesitate.

I called my friend back and asked her, "May I bless you today buy purchasing your plane ticket?"

She was so excited, "Oh, my GOD – would you please?"

...the rest is history! I felt so honored to bless someone during my time of need! May I share with you that originally, my flight to South Africa was $1,780; through GFM, I raised $2,600. Praise God!

We have an obligation as believers in Christ to help meet the needs of others. Obviously when we pray, recruiting the anointing of the Holy Spirit for guidance is most important. I encourage you to take a moment and evaluate where you are with the earnings that God has blessed you with. Are you sowing into the Kingdom? On fertile soil? If not, pray for wisdom, revelation-knowledge, and understanding.

VII

Responsible Budgeting

Scripture:

* **Proverbs 3:13-18** *"You're blessed when you meet Lady Wisdom; when you make friends with Madame insights. She's worth far more than money in the bank; her friendship is better than a big salary. Her value exceeds all the trappings of wealth; nothing you could wish for holds a candle to her. With one hand she gives long life, with the other she confesses recognition. Her manner is beautiful, her life wonderfully complete. She's the very Tree of Life to those who embrace her. Hold her tight – and be blessed"* (MSG).

🦋 **1 Timothy 6:10** *"For the love of money is the root of all evil: which while some coveted after, they have erred from the faith, and pierced themselves through with many sorrows."*

VIII

Sowing/Giving

Scripture:

- **Luke 6:38** *"Give, and it shall be given unto you; good measure, pressed down, and shaken together, and running over, shall men give into your bosom. For with the same measure that ye mete withal it shall be measured to you again."*

- **Luke 11: 9** *"And, I say unto you, Ask, and it shall be given to you; seek, and ye shall find; knock, and it shall be opened unto you."*

Part 4:

Scriptures for

Healing

Chapter 39:

Emotional Healing

Now that you've completed your wheel of transformation – let's take a look at a few scriptures, because the overall goal here is to encourage healing and it begins within…

Sin, abuse, neglect, rejection, and betrayal all cause great emotional and spiritual pain that hurt just like physical pain does. God our Great Physician can completely heal our broken hearts and bind our wounds, healing and making us whole. Spiritual and emotional healing is often a process with steps that we need to put action behind.

Use the following <u>Bible</u> verses to guide your heart and mind toward full recovery.

- *"My son, pay attention to what I say; turn your ear to my words. Do not let them out of your sight, keep* them within your heart; for they are life to those who find them and health to one's whole body."

~ **Proverbs 4:20-22**

- "A cheerful heart is good medicine, but a crushed spirit dries up the bones." ~ **Proverbs 17:22**

- "There is a time for everything, and a season for every activity under the heavens: a time to be born and a time to die, a time to plant and a time to uproot, a time to kill and a time to heal, a time to tear down and a time to build, a time to weep and a time to laugh, a time to mourn and a time to dance, a time to scatter stones and a time to gather them, a time to embrace and a time to refrain from embracing, a time to search and a time to give up, a time to keep and a time to throw away, a time to tear and a time to mend, a time to be silent and a time to speak, a time to love and a time to hate, a time for war and a time for peace." ~ **Ecclesiastes 3:1-8**

- "LORD, be gracious to us; we long for you. Be our strength every morning, our salvation in time of distress." ~ **Isaiah 33:2**

- "Therefore, confess your sins to each other and pray for each other so that you may be healed. The prayer of a righteous person is powerful and effective." ~ **James 5:6**

- "He himself bore our sins in his body on the cross, so that we might die to sins and live for righteousness; by his wounds you have been healed." ~ **1 Peter 2:24**

- *"Peace I leave with you; my peace I give you. I do not give to you as the world gives. Do not let your hearts be troubled and do not be afraid."* ~ **John 14:27**

- *"Come to me, all you who are weary and burdened, and I will give you rest. Take my yoke upon you and learn from me, for I am gentle and humble in heart, and you will find rest for your souls. For my yoke is easy and my burden is light."* ~ **Matthew 11:28-30**

- *"He gives strength to the weary and increases the power of the weak."* ~ **Isaiah 40:29**

- *"No temptation has overtaken you except what is common to mankind. And God is faithful; he will not let you be tempted beyond what you can bear. But when you are tempted, he will also provide a way out so that you can endure it.* " ~ **I Corinthians 10:13**

Chapter 40:

Physical Healing

- *"Heal me, O Lord, and I will be healed; save me and I will be saved, for you are the one I praise."*
  ~ Jeremiah 17:14

- *"Is anyone among you sick? Let them call the elders of the church to pray over them and anoint them with oil in the name of the Lord. And the prayer offered in faith will make the sick person well; the Lord will raise them up. If they have sinned, they will be forgiven."* **~ James 5:14-15**

- *"He said, 'If you listen carefully to the LORD your God and do what is right in his eyes, if you pay*

attention to his commands and keep all his decrees, I will not bring on you any of the diseases I brought on the Egyptians, for I am the LORD, who heals you.'"
~ Exodus 15:26

- "Worship the LORD your God, and his blessing will be on your food and water. I will take away sickness from among you..." **~ Exodus 23:25**

- "So, do not fear, for I am with you; do not be dismayed, for I am your God. I will strengthen you and help you; I will uphold you with my righteous right hand." **~ Isaiah 41:10**

- "Surely he took up our pain and bore our suffering, yet we considered him punished by God, stricken by him, and afflicted. But he was pierced for our transgressions, he was crushed for our iniquities; the punishment that brought us peace was on him, and by his wounds we are healed." ~ **Isaiah 53:4-5**

- "But I will restore you to health and heal your wounds; declares the LORD." ~ **Jeremiah 30:17**

- "See now that I myself am He! There is no god besides me. I put to death and I bring to life, I have wounded and I will heal, and no one can deliver out of my hand." ~ **Deuteronomy 32:39**

- "If my people, who are called by my name, will humble themselves and pray and seek my face and turn from their wicked ways, then I will hear from heaven, and I will forgive their sin and will heal their land. Now my eyes will be open and my ears attentive to the prayers offered in this place." ~ **2 Chronicles 7:14-15**

- "You restored me to health and let me live. Surely it was for my benefit that I suffered such anguish. In your love you kept me from the pit of destruction; you have put all my sins behind your back." ~ **Isaiah 38:16-17**

- "'I have seen their ways, but I will heal them; I will guide them and restore comfort to Israel's mourners, creating praise on their lips. Peace, peace, to those far and near,' says the LORD. 'And I will heal them.'" ~ **Isaiah 57:18-19**

- *"Nevertheless, I will bring health and healing to it; I will heal my people and will let them enjoy abundant peace and security."* ~ **Jeremiah 33:6**

- *"Dear friend, I pray that you may enjoy good health and that all may go well with you, even as your soul is getting along well."* ~ **3 John 1:2**

- *"And my God will meet all your needs according to the riches of his glory in Christ Jesus."* ~ **Philippians 4:19**

- *"He will wipe every tear from their eyes. There will be no more death' or mourning or crying or pain, for the old order of things has passed away."* ~ **Revelations 21:4**

Part 5:

Final

Thoughts

I close this journey offering a Psalm of David, written as an appeal to God for Guidance and Deliverance. Thank you for spending time with me, I pray that my assignment has been successfully completed, and I trust in the name of God that you are walking in your healing – today! I love you dearly, and I trust that we will meet again - soon! Until then, rest in the knowledge of the Word; seek God's guidance daily! Evaluate your circle of influence and gravitate to the things of God – you'll know what they are. Quiet your soul and setting into the responsibilities given to you for this time – it will be through integrity and excellence that you will achieve what God has set before you; keep in mind that the realm of the Spirit will be reflected in your natural environment.

Psalm 143

New King James Version

Hear my prayer, O LORD,

Give ear to my supplications!

In Your faithfulness answer me,

And in Your righteousness.

Do not enter into judgment with Your
servant,

For in Your sight no one living is
righteous.

For the enemy has persecuted my soul;

He has crushed my life to the ground;

He has made me dwell in¹darkness,

Like those who have long been dead.

Therefore my spirit is overwhelmed within

me;

My heart within me is distressed.

I remember the days of old;

I meditate on all Your works;

I muse on the work of Your hands.

I spread out my hands to You;

My soul longs for You like a thirsty

land. Selah

Answer me speedily, O LORD;

My spirit fails!

Do not hide Your face from me,

Lest I be like those who go down into

the pit.

Cause me to hear Your loving-kindness in

the morning,

For in You do I trust;

Cause me to know the way in which I

should walk,

For I lift up my soul to You.

Deliver me, O LORD, from my enemies;

In You I take shelter.

Teach me to do Your will,

For You are my God;

Your Spirit is good.

Lead me in the land of uprightness.

Revive me, O LORD, for Your name's

sake!

For Your righteousness' sake bring my

soul out of trouble.

In Your mercy cut off my enemies,

And destroy all those who afflict my soul;

For I am Your servant.

Chapter 41:

National Domestic Violence Hotline

If you are being physically abused, please get help!

- Call 911, or
- The *National Domestic Violence Hotline* at 800-799-7233 and talk with an advocate.

Do not remain in an abusive relationship. You are not at fault for a man hitting you and any man who blames you for his lack of self-control does not deserve you. You are better, you are beautifully anointed, and you must believe in your value.

Acknowledgments

I honor my amazingly handsome husband, Montez, who works effortlessly with me to create a loving environment where we worship together and exercise unconditional love. Thank you for your willingness to travel on this journey with me – I am blessed to have you as my husband, my priest, and my handsome angel.

To my loving daughters, Darreial and DeJasma "Jazz," I am so proud of the women that you are today! I am thankful to God for trusting me with you. I often reflect on how strong you were for me during your childhood years. Every waking moment with you gave me another ounce of hope! Thank you for every smile, every laugh, every hug, and every word of encouragement. You were my driving force for living, and it's because of you that my strength increased – you inspired me to muster up the courage to share the most intimate details of my life. I've always told you that I've been hurt enough for all of us – you never have to hurt again, my precious babies. You are special! Your feelings are important! You are valuable! You are a beautiful woman of God. This book is dedicated to you – be free; fly on the wings of God's anointing!

To my equally amazing grandchildren - Za'Naudia, Za'Moria, Millah, Hashan, and Harmony – my extended DNA, always Nana's babies! I see a little bit of me in all of you. You shine as examples of God's anointing over my life, and I decree by faith that chains are broken – our family has been healed, delivered and restored. May the Grace of our Almighty Father in Heaven continue to meet your every need! May you continue to do well, walk in the fruit of the Spirit, and remember to love unconditionally.

Deniece William's, "Black Butterfly" (Sing Along)

Morning light, silken dream take flight
As the darkness gave way to the dawn
You've survived, now your moment has
arrived
Now your dream has finally been born

Black butterfly sailed across the waters
Tell your sons and daughters what the
struggle brings
Black butterfly set the skies on fire

Rise up even higher so the ageless winds of
time can catch your wings

Ooh...ooh...

While you slept, the promise was unkept
But your faith was as sure as the stars
Now you're free and the world has come to
see
Just how proud and beautiful you are
Black butterfly sail across the waters
Tell your sons and daughters what the
struggle brings
Black butterfly set the skies on fire
Rise up even higher so the wind can catch
your wings
Let the current lift your heart and send it
soaring
Write your timeless message clear across
the sky

So that all of us can read it and
remember when we need it
That a dream conceived in truth can
never die
Butterfly

`Cause now that you're free and the world
has come to see
Just how proud and beautiful you are

Black butterfly sail across the waters
Tell your sons and your daughters what
the struggle brings
Black butterfly set the skies
Rise up even higher so the ageless winds of
time can catch your wings
Fly
Butterfly
Yeah, yeah, yes
Fly

References

New King James Version (NKJV). Copyright 1982, Thomas Nelson.

https://www.biblegateway.com/passage/?search=psalm+143&version=NKJV

Black Butterfly: Deniece Williams, Google.

https://www.google.com/search?newwindow=1&safe=active&source=hp&ei=RAxlXejTA4aZ_QaLqK3wCQ&q=black+butterfly+lyrics&oq=black+butter&gs_l=psy-ab.1.3.35i39j0l9.504.8195..11360...8.0..0.101.1559.21j1.....0....1..gws-wiz.....10..0i131.6LebyzqInlk#spf=1566903372537

74540545R00107

Made in the USA
Columbia, SC
16 September 2019